BE YOUR OWN BOAT
SURVEYOR

Published by Adlard Coles Nautical
an imprint of Bloomsbury Publishing Plc
50 Bedford Square, London WC1B 3DP
www.adlardcoles.com

Bloomsbury is a trademark of Bloomsbury Publishing Plc

Copyright © Dag Pike 2014

First published by Adlard Coles Nautical in 2014

ISBN 978-1-4729-0367-9
ePDF 978-1-4729-0369-3
ePub 978-1-4729-0368-6

The right of the author to be identified as the author
of this work has been asserted by him in accordance
with the Copyright, Designs and Patents Act, 1988.

A CIP catalogue record for this book is available from
the British Library.

This book is produced using paper that is made from
wood grown in managed, sustainable forests. It is
natural, renewable and recyclable. The logging and
manufacturing processes conform to the environmental
regulations of the country of origin.

Designed by Austin Taylor
Typeset in Griffith Gothic

Printed and bound in China by Toppan Leefung Printing

Note: while all reasonable care has been taken in
the publication of this book, the publisher takes no
responsibility for the use of the methods or products
described in the book.

10 9 8 7 6 5 4 3 2 1

BE YOUR OWN BOAT
SURVEYOR

A hands-on guide for all owners and buyers

DAG PIKE

ADLARD COLES NAUTICAL

B L O O M S B U R Y

LONDON • NEW DELHI • NEW YORK • SYDNEY

PUBLISHED IN ASSOCIATION WITH  **PANTAENIUS**
Sail & Motor Yacht Insurance

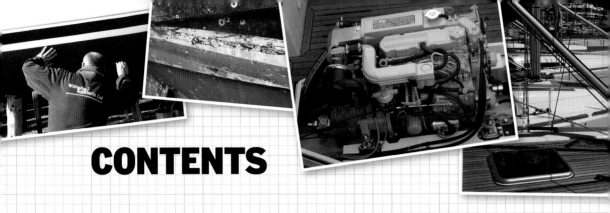

CONTENTS

1 WHY SURVEY YOUR OWN BOAT?

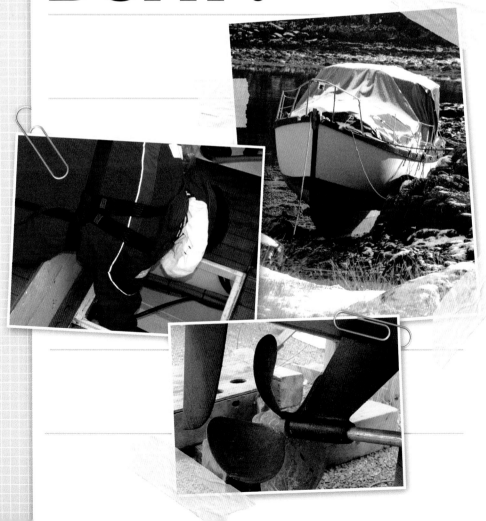

WHY SURVEY
YOUR OWN BOAT?

THE TOOLS
OF THE TRADE

THE
HULL

DECK AND
SUPERSTRUCTURE

ENGINES AND
THEIR SYSTEMS

STERN
GEAR

PLUMBING

UNLESS YOU'RE IN the market for buying a second hand boat, it's not usually good news when you have to call in a surveyor. They may be brought in to assess damage to your boat after an accident, or the insurance company might demand a survey when your boat reaches a certain age (usually around ten years) just to be sure about its condition. When you are buying second hand you certainly want a survey done before you commit. So the surveyor's job, whether it is a purchase or insurance survey, is to use his specialist experience and skill to go through the boat with a fine-tooth comb, find any problems and propose solutions. For a damage survey the motivation is obvious but the surveyor will also assess the general condition in case that falls below what might be considered to be an insurable standard.

To a certain extent the surveyor is a bit like a detective. He will crawl round inside and outside the boat inspecting the fittings, fixtures and the hull itself to find the clues that will determine whether the boat is in sound condition or where any problems lie. It can be a difficult job at times because these clues are sometimes quite small and apparently insignificant, and it is only by putting them all together that the surveyor can assess the condition of the boat. He will use sight, feel, often smell and sometimes instruments to determine what may be wrong. It can be a challenging but fascinating job and, like so many jobs of this nature, it's a constant learning curve, as construction methods and materials for boats develop.

When damage has occurred or when the insurance or finance company has demanded a survey, you will want to use a professional surveyor. You will probably also want to employ a surveyor to give you a report before you make a final decision on your next boat, but a good quality survey does not come cheap. If you're considering several boats before finally deciding on the one you want, you could

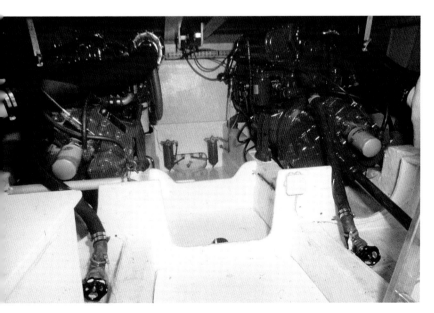

← *Checking your own boat means delving into all those areas that you don't usually see.*

↑ *The stern gear is one of the most critical areas to check because it is normally underwater and out of reach.*

↑ *This deterioration may be only cosmetic but it is advisable to take a closer look.*

run up a considerable bill. Owners will want to carry out their own survey to avoid such costs where possible.

Carrying out a survey on a boat has always been something of a mysterious art and there is no doubt that skill and experience is required. However if you are prepared to get a boiler suit on and enter the normally unseen parts of a boat you can carry out a survey yourself. You may not have the professional experience but there are usually plenty of clues to help you pinpoint areas of concern. This book is aimed at the owner or potential owner who wants to be able to carry out a basic survey. It should help you find potential problems in your own boat and get them fixed before they become serious. And if you're buying, it should guide you through the survey process with enough information to decide whether to go ahead with the purchase and get the professional in (or walk on to the next boat on your list).

The buyer's survey

WHEN YOU ARE buying a second hand boat there is no reason why you should not do your own preliminary survey. You may not discover all the problems that a professional would but

WHY SURVEY
YOUR OWN BOAT?

THE TOOLS
OF THE TRADE

THE
HULL

DECK AND
SUPERSTRUCTURE

ENGINES AND
THEIR SYSTEMS

STERN
GEAR

PLUMBING

↙ If you are thinking of buying a boat you should see it out of the water if possible.

↑ There are many parts of the rigging that need checking in detail.

at least you should be able to spot areas of concern that may convince you to avoid a certain boat. By discovering problems at this early stage of the buying process you can rule out some of your potential purchases yourself, and save a great deal of money on professional surveys before you find a boat that looks to be in a suitable and reasonable condition and warrants a professional opinion (both to reassure yourself and possibly your finance company and insurer).

There will rarely be time for you to do a full survey when you are assessing potential purchases; the yacht broker or the owner isn't likely to want you to spend hours crawling around their boats. If you want to look at several boats before deciding, you need to be able to do a sort of preliminary survey, one that should throw up any major faults or at least give you an idea of how the boat has been maintained over the years. Chapter 13 gives you the tools with which to do this. Professional surveyors may throw up their hands in horror at this approach but it is a pragmatic solution to what could be quite a difficult problem for potential purchasers. It is no substitute for a much more detailed survey, either by you or a professional, but it should enable you to decide whether to take a more detailed look at a boat or walk away.

If you have done your own survey on a boat and identified faults that you are reasonably comfortable with and willing to accept when you make the purchase, you will also have a yardstick to judge the quality of the professional surveyor's report. Hopefully he will have noted all the things that you found wrong and probably a few more besides, but you are now in a position to make a judgement about the quality of his survey if he doesn't uncover some of the issues that you found. It has been known.

The owner's survey

IF YOU ARE already the proud owner of a boat then being able to carry out a survey yourself can be very rewarding. This could be something that you do on an annual basis, perhaps just before you lay it up for the winter. You will probably already have a list of things that need attention

↑ At a quick glance it looks to be in good order but you do need to look very closely at the detail.

↓ Make sure that the hull is well supported and accessible before starting the checks.

WHY SURVEY
YOUR OWN BOAT?

THE TOOLS
OF THE TRADE

THE
HULL

DECK AND
SUPERSTRUCTURE

ENGINES AND
THEIR SYSTEMS

STERN
GEAR

PLUMBING

↑ Access to all parts of the boat is desirable when doing a survey.

↓ It is much easier to check the mast and rigging when it is lowered.

but this will develop from what you see and learn from operating the boat. If you spend a morning doing your own survey, not only will you be able to put together a more comprehensive list of things that need fixing but you'll also have a lot more confidence in your boat the next season. Furthermore, not only will you get to know what makes your boat tick, but this detailed knowledge will stand you in good stead should you experience an emergency out at sea. If you find the water levels rising inside the boat in lively seas you'll have a much better idea of where to look for trouble, how to get access quickly and where the seacocks and the piping are. Everybody should know their boat in this detailed way but in practice very few do. When you have an emergency on your hands and quick action is needed, the last thing you want to be doing is getting the manual out and flicking through its pages. Of course, if you do a survey you should be less at risk of having an emergency at sea in the first place.

Getting access

WHEN YOU'RE CARRYING out a survey you can only examine what you can see. This may sound like stating the obvious, but a professional surveyor's report itemises the areas where examinations have been carried out and where lack of access has made this impossible. He does this to cover himself because you cannot give a blanket assurance that all is well unless you have inspected every single part of the boat, and in most cases this is just not possible because of the way it has been put together.

Modern yachts tend to be assembled for the convenience of the builder rather than to give the owner or surveyor access: the trend is to fit an inner moulding inside the main hull moulding, so unless you cut sections out there is simply no way to inspect the hidden areas inside. The professional surveyor covers himself by using phrases in his report such as 'the hull was in sound condition where examined'.

You have to do much the same when it comes to undertaking your own examination. Obviously, open up all the hatches and access panels as far as you can and if you find that the bits you can see are sound, you can be reasonably comfortable

↓ *You do need to look very closely and in detail at the inside of a steel hull.*

WHY SURVEY
YOUR OWN BOAT?

THE TOOLS
OF THE TRADE

THE
HULL

DECK AND
SUPERSTRUCTURE

ENGINES AND
THEIR SYSTEMS

STERN
GEAR

PLUMBING

↑ When the boat is being built access to the inside of the hull is possible, but this access can be restricted once built.

↑ An old fashioned hull with copper plating over the wood that can make access to the hull challenging.

that the hidden areas are sound too. It's not a 100 per cent guarantee but it's the best you can do short of ripping the boat apart. To overcome some of the access problems the professional can use mirrors and/or cameras. A mirror on a stick, rather like an overgrown dentist's mirror, allows the surveyor to see into many hidden areas. Using it, and getting light into the area, does take some skill but it does help to open up areas that would otherwise be hidden.

I used this technique once when there was a leak from a generator exhaust pipe hidden behind the fuel tank, and the camera showed up the salt encrustation that was a sure sign of a leak. While it didn't provide the cure, at least we knew what the problem was.

You can also do a survey when a boat is afloat, but you won't be able to do a full job. Bear in mind that your survey is aimed at checking the areas of the boat that

you don't normally see. This includes the underwater areas, and as fittings such as the propeller and the rudder can be vital to your safety these should be a priority in any survey. You'll need to get a close look at how fair the hull shape is so that any distortions are apparent. On a sailboat you also need to be able to inspect the keel or centreboard. This is where wear and tear can occur without you being immediately aware of it, so get the boat on dry land, preferably on a hard standing and securely chocked up, because you will be crawling underneath it.

Surveying skills

WHAT SKILLS DO you need to carry out your own survey? First you need to be reasonably agile, because you'll be crawling in and out of tight spaces. Most boats were never designed with easy access to the hidden parts in mind – when

13

I was surveying, I often found it relatively easy to get inside a compartment but much trickier to get out again! – so you have to make the best access provisions that you can and, again, you can only survey what you can see.

You need to use all your senses on the survey, except perhaps taste, but the most important attribute is having the patience to carry out such close examination. Of course experience counts when doing a survey, but what it mainly does is allow you to quickly find the source of a problem. A professional surveyor develops the instinct to anticipate certain faults, but those new to surveying need to go slow; it is all too easy to give areas of the hull a cursory glance and think that you have checked them out but this won't catch the often tiny clues: minute cracks or discolouration that should make you stop and explore the area in a bit more detail.

When you are surveying your own boat you may find it harder to be objective. At

WHY SURVEY YOUR OWN BOAT?

THE TOOLS OF THE TRADE

THE HULL

DECK AND SUPERSTRUCTURE

ENGINES AND THEIR SYSTEMS

STERN GEAR

PLUMBING

← *Don't forget to include the tender as part of your survey.*

→ *The engine may be past its sell-by date but the hull may still be sound.*

↙ *Conditions like this could make it difficult for a detailed survey.*

the back of your mind is the thought that you don't really want to find any problems because you'll then have to deal with them, and that's likely to cost you money. But you should resist the temptation to gloss over areas and, believe me, it can be quite tricky. It's so easy to pretend that there isn't a problem when you don't want to see it, and I have come across owners who have even installed new fittings onto sections of the boat that were deteriorating.

When you do come across something you don't understand or which looks like it may require a significant repair, it's time to call in the experts, maybe an independent surveyor who can give his opinion or a boatyard you want to approach about the repair. I would like to think that the boatyard opinion, as well as being free, would be unbiased but they may be keen to get the work, so they're not always completely objective. You will have to pay for an independent view from a surveyor and, like most things in life, you get what

you pay for. If you spot a problem on a boat that you are considering buying, the simple solution is to walk away and continue your search elsewhere.

This is the pessimistic view and there is every chance your own survey won't throw up any major problems. Instead it should give you the confidence that you know how everything works and operates and that your boat is sound for another season. A boat is a very personal thing and carrying out a detailed survey will enhance your relationship with it.

2 THE TOOLS OF THE TRADE

WHY SURVEY YOUR OWN BOAT?

THE TOOLS OF THE TRADE

THE HULL

DECK AND SUPERSTRUCTURE

ENGINES AND THEIR SYSTEMS

STERN GEAR

PLUMBING

THE TOOLS YOU need for carrying out your own survey are very simple and the chances are you'll already have most of them. You might see the professional surveyor carrying a hefty tool box around with him but he has to cater for every possible requirement, and your survey will follow a more simple route. Before we look at the actual physical tools it is worth reiterating that some of the most important assets for assessing the condition of a boat are your five senses, so let's have a quick look at how you use them.

Using your senses

OF ALL THE senses, touch is probably the most important to the surveyor. Run your fingers lightly over a hull or deck surface and you'll quickly become aware of imperfections, roughness or distortions. You may be able to feel an area of slight change or rise in the surface where a repair has been carried out on a composite hull and the old and new material joins. You will certainly be able to feel chips and scratches. When you're checking out the wire rigging on a sailboat (wearing a pair of good leather gloves) you're running your hands up and down the wire to try and find any broken wires.

Sight is probably as critical as touch when it comes to first detecting then analysing any problems. A professional surveyor's first step may be to simply stand and look at the boat, and with experience you may also learn where to look for trouble spots without even getting close to the boat. Look for tiny cracks, changes in colour or other imperfections. A magnifying glass helps, especially when examining the reinforcing material below the gel coat on a composite hull, so make it part of your tool kit. Binoculars also help you to get a closer look at difficult areas such as the top of the mast, if this is erected during the survey. You might also want to use mirrors in one form or another (see page 19). Sight is also your first line of defence if there is a distortion in the hull: do both sides look the same and is the rudder in line with the keel? Anything that seems a bit out of kilter should be suspect (it is easy to overlook such major discrepancies when focusing on the finer points of a boat's structure).

Sound comes into play as you assess the hull and fittings because you can use light taps with a hammer (or even your knuckles) to identify areas with a different composition (such as 'sandwich' construction) and possible deterioration: good condition material should 'ring', while suspect material gives off a softer, duller sound. This simple technique works on many parts of a boat, including the hulls and decks of composite boats, keels and keel bolts and in fact most parts of the structure that should be rigid and taut. Even a wooden hull should have that same sort of 'ringing' sound if it's in good condition.

Every boat has a unique smell, which may be compounded by water in the bilges, styrene in the laminate of a composite moulding (although this is only likely in newer boats), rot in a wooden hull, leaking toilets and other outlets, engine and diesel oil, and many other causes. You need experience to successfully exploit your sense of smell during a survey, but once you've seen dry rot, you'll remember what it smells like for a long time! So don't ignore your nose; even if at first you can't identify the smell, take the trouble to try and pin down the cause because in most cases a bad or noxious smell indicates some form of defect – there was a time when boats would smell of the materials used in their construction, such as pitch and tar, but apart from the styrene smell, a new boat should be free from significant odours.

Using your sense of taste is something you want to do with considerable care, and only to differentiate between fresh and salt water to help determine where a leak is coming from. However, any water on board can be contaminated so tasting it should be a last resort. Certainly if we were to exclude one of the senses from the investigative process, this is the one, so use it at your own discretion.

There can also be a sort of sixth sense, a 'gut feeling' that indicates potential trouble ahead for a particular boat. It may be hard to put your finger on just what it is, but don't ignore the warning signs – they're usually right.

Tools

NOW IT'S TIME to turn our attention to the hardware a surveyor might use. The aim of any survey is to assess the condition of the boat without causing further damage, so bear this in mind when choosing the right tools for the job.

A light hammer, perhaps one used for knocking in tacks, is great for non-destructive testing because you can tap your way around the boat and get a good feel for its condition with relative ease. Some surveyors use a brass or a hard plastic hammer to reduce the chance of damage, but not only are these difficult to find, I don't think they offer much over a normal steel hammer. You only need to tap lightly to get the right kind of feedback: let the hammer bounce on the hull surface or on a bolt head and listen to the 'ring' (or otherwise). If you are surveying a steel hull you may need to chip away rust; a hammer with a 'chipping head' will do the job.

Some sort of spike or pricker can be useful for exploring the depths of a crack

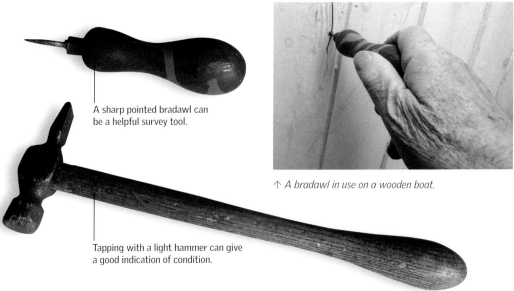

A sharp pointed bradawl can be a helpful survey tool.

↑ A bradawl in use on a wooden boat.

Tapping with a light hammer can give a good indication of condition.

↑ The bradawl/pricker could be useful here to test the wood around the fastenings.

in composite gel coat, perhaps, or for checking wooden structures for soft areas that may indicate rot. Again, you don't need anything big and heavy: I use a bradawl with a point about 2cm (0.8in) long. A small screwdriver would do, provided it has a decent sized handle, but you could also grind down the end of a larger screwdriver, both of which will enable you to poke around in tight areas. Because you'll be using both the hammer and spike frequently during surveys, fit them with comfortable handles.

A scraper can be useful for removing marine growth on the hull or stern gear, or perhaps for exposing the actual hull surface beneath the antifouling paint on the underwater part of the hull. Again, it doesn't need to be large; a small paint scraper will do the job, but make sure it's not a three-pointed 'triangular' scraper designed for pull scraping rather than pushing, as this can easily scratch the hull. Supplement the scraper with a small brush with stiff nylon bristles, which is useful for cleaning surfaces you want to inspect more closely.

A ruler or measuring tape helps when sizing up areas of damage or decay, or to pinpoint problems for further expert assessment. Unless you are diligent and write down everything as you find it, you might want to have some sort of narrow masking tape to mark off problem areas. If you can write on the tape, even better – I've found the masking tape supplied to decorators for edge painting works well; it sticks to most surfaces and is easily removed without damage. It can also be useful for dividing the hull surface into small sections, meaning you'll be far less likely to miss a spot.

As we have already discussed, getting as much access as possible to the inside of the hull, especially engine and steering compartments and hidden bilge areas, is an important part of any survey. Be sure to get permission from the owner or broker before you start unscrewing panels – you don't want to be accused of damage to any part of the boat. Where there is no visible access, other than by a hand or arm, there are two options. The first is a mirror mounted on a stick, and you can purchase these in various forms or rig one up yourself. The second is a camera. While the mirror allows you to see hidden areas and make your assessment on the spot, a modern digital camera is more compact, and can provide vital illumination and a permanent record of any damage you discover. A camera with a moveable angle viewing screen is even better, as it allows you to assess the 'hidden' area from different angles.

While a digital camera offers some light, it is not enough to undertake a thorough survey, so a torch is a must. I use one with

WHY SURVEY YOUR OWN BOAT?

THE TOOLS OF THE TRADE

THE HULL

DECK AND SUPERSTRUCTURE

ENGINES AND THEIR SYSTEMS

STERN GEAR

PLUMBING

↑ *Good lighting is essential when delving into the bilges.*

LED bulbs, which give a good white light, and the brighter the better. Other elements to consider include the ability to adjust the light from wide angle to pinpoint, and a free-standing or head-mount option to free up both hands should you need to tend to a problem. Of course, if there is a mains supply of electricity on board, you can use a wandering lead to give a brighter light.

If you are surveying a stainless steel boat you may need a magnet to test hull quality. Good quality stainless steel should be non-magnetic, although there are still some good grades that are slightly magnetic, meaning it's not a completely sound test (see chapter 3 for more information on stainless steel hulls).

MOISTURE METERS
– PROS AND CONS

Many surveyors have taken to using moisture meters to help them determine whether any water has been absorbed into the hull laminate. Water absorption can be a major problem for hull and deck laminates, particularly those that feature a core between the inner and outer layers, the so-called 'sandwich construction'. If water gets into this core the laminate starts to break down, with the core separating from the outer skins and the hull or deck structure becoming weaker and less rigid, which could lead to costly repairs or even the scrapping of the boat as the only cure. This nightmare scenario has plagued the boat industry for years, and is largely down to the poor construction methods and materials of the past. But a moisture meter may help you to detect if there is a problem of this nature.

Note the emphases – using a moisture meter to get a reliable reading can be a bit of a minefield and is something usually best left to the professionals. However, if you

↓ *A moisture meter can be a useful condition guide for the hull, but the readings need careful interpretation.*

are determined to try it, there are several requirements that need to be met before you run the test. First, there are many moisture meters on the market, most of them designed for use on buildings rather than boats. You obviously want to purchase a meter that is specifically designed for boats, and they're not cheap. Next, the hull should be out of the water and must be given time to dry out (the planking on a wooden hull is unlikely to fully dry out, making a moisture meter reading less meaningful, although on a cold-moulded wooden hull the wood should be impervious to water uptake). Don't be tempted to take the reading from the outside of the boat – you will get a more reliable reading from the inside, so be sure that it is also dry and free of water stains, which suggest water has been lying in the bilge. Moreover, rain or even a damp atmosphere can distort results, so take the weather conditions into account before attempting a reading. Finally, you need a good dose of experience to perform a reliable test and interpret the results. Get all this right and annual moisture tests (in comparable atmospheric conditions and after the same period of drying time) can be a good indication of any deterioration in the laminate.

However, moisture meters are often more trouble than they're worth and even the professionals struggle with them. On this basis it's probably wise to steer clear of them when conducting a personal survey and instead concentrate on the more obvious signs of water ingress into the laminate, such as staining (we will look at this in more detail in chapter 3).

Finally, since you will be spending a lot of time on your knees, crawling through the

↑ *The moisture meter can be used on wood as well.*

nether regions of a boat, you might want to wear suitable clothing such as a boiler suit and possibly a pair of knee pads to ease stresses and strains.

So now you have your basic tool kit, the survey can begin.

Keeping a record

RECORD YOUR FINDINGS as soon as possible – it's easy to forget the various defects in just one compartment, and even harder to keep it all straight in your head if you're surveying several boats in one day. We have already discussed the use of a digital camera, but it is also imperative to keep a list. Some surveyors use an electronic recorder and transcribe their findings after they've completed the survey, but I like pen and paper because you tend to remember things better once you've

WHY SURVEY YOUR OWN BOAT?

THE TOOLS OF THE TRADE

THE HULL

DECK AND SUPERSTRUCTURE

ENGINES AND THEIR SYSTEMS

STERN GEAR

PLUMBING

written them down, plus there is also the possibility that your notes will include clues that will aid your investigation (for example, you might spot a defect on the outside of the boat that needs checking from the inside; your notes won't let you forget it!). It's not always easy to fiddle about with a pen when you have greasy or wet hands, so consider using a personal shorthand to speed things up (as long as you remember what the shorthand means!).

↑ Good access to the hull is a vital element of a survey.

↓ Wooden supports should be checked carefully before going under a hull.

ACCESS

As we have discussed, the more access you have to a boat the better the survey. A ladder or steps will allow you to get up close and personal with the surfaces you're inspecting. With smaller boats up to 10 metres it may be possible to access the topsides from the ground, but you will still need to examine the deck and carry out your hammer 'tap testing', so climb aboard.

Getting under the boat is of equal importance and, since you'll be spending a large portion of your time beneath the hull, you want to be sure that the boat is securely supported. Sailboats are often cradled on an adjustable metal stand and provided that all of the bolts and fittings are in place, it should be secure because the keel will actually be sitting on part of the framework. Take a critical eye to boats supported by baulks of timber and wedges or even old oil drums, which could come loose as you work.

A sailboat with a fixed keel should sit well off the ground with easy access to those parts of the hull normally below the waterline. Even so, you might have to lie on the ground to see the bottom of the keel or the rudder. With a motorboat it will usually be resting on its keel, perhaps on blocks of wood, and so you'll need to crawl under the boat to inspect the underwater parts of the

↓ Access to sailboat hulls is usually good.

WHY SURVEY YOUR OWN BOAT?

THE TOOLS OF THE TRADE

THE HULL

DECK AND SUPERSTRUCTURE

ENGINES AND THEIR SYSTEMS

STERN GEAR

PLUMBING

Tool checklist

- ☐ Light hammer
- ☐ Pricker/bradawl
- ☐ Scraper
- ☐ Small brush with stiff nylon bristles
- ☐ Mirror on a stick
- ☐ Digital camera
- ☐ Torch
- ☐ Moisture meter
- ☐ Magnet (for steel hulls)
- ☐ Pen and notebook, or recorder
- ☐ Access to ladder or steps

hull, not a pleasant experience on a wet day but that is one of the 'joys' of surveying! These are the areas that need close scrutiny so you do need to get right under there if you are going to feel comfortable that you've found all possible problems.

3 THE HULL

THE HULL IS obviously the most vital
component of a boat. Any failure here
can lead to catastrophic consequences,
and any necessary repair work can be both
expensive and sometimes very difficult to
carry out, so it should be your main focus
in a survey.

The hull can take a lot of punishment
both at sea and in harbour, and the
designer and builder have to tread a
narrow line between making the structure
strong enough to withstand wear and tear
while also keeping it as light as possible
(the weight of a hull can be critical on
planing powerboats or performance
sailboats). The designer should always err
on the side of safety and augment strength,
just to be sure. This is good news for an
owner, since hull strength can reduce with
age. You'll need to decide how extensive
the deterioration is and how much it has
affected hull strength overall, which is
somewhat problematic as many of the
signs can be well hidden at first sight,
meaning a subtle approach is required.

↓ *This centreboard hull would need to be checked
thoroughly for all the parts and fittings.*

Stresses on the hull structure

TO HELP YOU understand the hull
structure and how it is designed,
think about the stresses the hull has to
withstand. On a planing motorboat the
bottom of the hull can suffer very high
impact loadings as it pounds through
waves, which causes flexing of the bottom
panels. There is also considerable stress on
the transom or stern areas, which have to
accommodate the considerable thrust of
the propellers. Displacement motorboats
face much less stress and weight is less
critical in this type of boat, so there
shouldn't be any problems relating to
structural strength, although the fastenings
on a wooden boat can be a weak point.

While in sailboats some stress
originates from wave impact, it is the
rigging that imposes the main stresses on
the hull. The shrouds pull upwards on both
sides of the hull at the attachment points
and there are similar strains at the bow
and stern where the forestay and backstays
try to pull the ends of the boat upwards.

WHY SURVEY
YOUR OWN BOAT?

THE TOOLS
OF THE TRADE

THE
HULL

DECK AND
SUPERSTRUCTURE

ENGINES AND
THEIR SYSTEMS

STERN
GEAR

PLUMBING

At the same time, the mast is pressing down in the centre, meaning the hull has to act something like a rigid girder to take the strain. The keel can add further stress as its weight hangs down to balance some of the force generated by the wind in the sails.

By visualising these stresses, it is somewhat easier to understand the risk attached to any defects you may find in the hull structure. A failure of some sort around the area of the shroud attachments, for example, could be quite serious, while small areas of osmosis (see page 32) on the hull surface might look bad at first but are quickly resolved with cosmetic attention.

Hull construction materials

IF YOU'RE NOT the owner of the boat, one of the first things you'll need to determine in any survey is the type of hull you're dealing with, and it's not always obvious. There are three main types of hull construction materials: composite, wood and metal. Within these main types there are subdivisions. Examples of composite hulls include sandwich construction, solid laminate, vacuum infusion and hulls with internal liners. Wooden hulls include traditional plank on frame constructions, plywood panels, triple diagonal planking, cold moulded hulls and clinker planking, all in a wide variety of woods. There are essentially two metals – steel and aluminium – used to construct metal hulls, and these certainly have different corrosion characteristics. Metal hulls are generally welded but you may come across older riveted hulls where thin aluminium is present. (There are hulls constructed from ferro-cement, but these are virtually impossible to survey since you'd have to cut out a section of the hull to assess its construction quality, and then you'd only

↓ Ferro-cement hulls are quite rare these days and it is very difficult to assess their condition from a survey.

be assessing one section. However, if rust from the metal armature is showing on the surface, walk away.)

If you're struggling to identify the material of the hull, seek out the boat builders or search for boat reviews or brochures on the internet: you'll need to know what you're looking at as the surveying techniques are very different for each material, which you'll discover when you read on.

Common features

DISTORTION

Before we look at the techniques for surveying different types of hull, let's look at their common features. The first thing you should consider is the fairness of the hull, so before you even get up close to the boat have a good look at it from a distance. From the end of a sailboat, are the mast, hull and keel, and rudder in line? Do both sides of the boat look even? From the side, do the lines of the chines and deck – and on powered craft, the keel – run in smooth, flowing curves?

Signs of distortion on a wooden boat suggest it hasn't been supported adequately when out of the water, while distortion in a metal hull is more likely to be a construction problem. Composite hulls are less prone to distortion, so if anything is out of line it could be the result of damage or poor moulding techniques, more common on older craft but still present in modern craft that have been built down in price rather than up in quality. If the mast is out of line with the hull this could influence the adjustment of the rigging screws on each side.

↑ *Looking along the side of the hull can show up any irregularities.*

↓ *This fire damage is obvious from the outside but there is likely to be extensive damage inside.*

KEEL

One of the more important areas to examine on the outside of sailboats is the keel attachment. Today most keels are made from cast steel and they don't always sit comfortably with the hull, meaning you may see a line of corrosion or even a small gap where the two meet. This would be a cause for concern because it suggests

WHY SURVEY YOUR OWN BOAT?

THE TOOLS OF THE TRADE

THE HULL

DECK AND SUPERSTRUCTURE

ENGINES AND THEIR SYSTEMS

STERN GEAR

PLUMBING

that water has got between the hull and the keel and the expansion caused by the corrosion could put pressure on the keel bolts. The only way to be sure is to lower the keel and check what is happening in the gap. The corrosion could extend to the keel bolts themselves, but much would depend on the metal they are made from. Modern yachts mainly use stainless steel bolts, which should not corrode provided the right sort of stainless steel is used. Bronze and galvanised steel bolts featured in the past and certainly the latter can corrode, perhaps through electrolytic action, if the galvanising wears off. If you see such signs of corrosion emanating from the joint between the keel and the hull it could also signal that there is corrosion on the top surface of the steel keel; I'd suggest lowering or removing the keel to get to the root cause. If the keel bolts are accessible from the inside of the hull, tap them with your hammer: you should get a hard ring if they're in sound condition, although there are no guarantees with this test when you're assessing a lead keel, which can deaden the sound.

There are many different types of keels on sailboats, including fin, drop and bulb

↓ *This head of a keel bolt inside the hull, showing signs of corrosion, demands close examination.*

↑ *A sailboat keel ready for refitting after being lowered for inspection.*

→ *Keel bolts are fitted to metal keels. Corrosion can occur in the concealed areas if water gets in.*

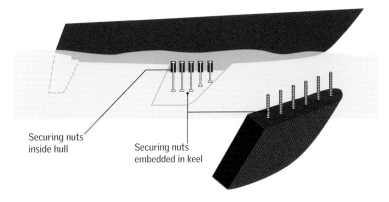

Securing nuts inside hull

Securing nuts embedded in keel

↑ *Signs of leaking from the hull/keel joint of a sailboat.*

↑ *Corrosion showing in the hull/keel joint of a sailboat.*

keels, and these all have different methods of attachment. Since this is an area that is critical to safety you don't want to take chances here. Go over the attachments and the joints with an eagle eye to ensure there are no signs of movement or corrosion, either inside or out.

SIGNS OF GROUNDING
The keel is also the first part of the boat to touch bottom in the event of a grounding so look for signs of abrasion or gouging around its bottom. Grounding can put a very heavy stress on the keel/hull joint and its attachment and this could be the reason for that corrosion in the attachment joint.

If you're surveying a motorboat you also want to be looking for similar signs of past grounding, but in the stern area, which is usually the deepest part of the hull when the boat is afloat. Propellers and rudders can often be the first point of contact on a planing boat, while on a displacement hull it will usually be the keel towards the stern.

Displacement motorboats often have a skeg along the bottom of the hull, which takes the impact of any grounding and protects the hull itself. If a metal shoe is fitted to the skeg look for signs of distortion or strain in the attachment bolts and general abrasion and if you find them, it's time for a closer look. The metal shoes are usually made from steel and it's not

↓ *The paint has been ground back on this hull/keel joint to examine the extent of the corrosion problem.*

↓ *This fin keel is showing signs that the yacht has grounded at some point in its life.*

WHY SURVEY YOUR OWN BOAT?

THE TOOLS OF THE TRADE

THE HULL

DECK AND SUPERSTRUCTURE

ENGINES AND THEIR SYSTEMS

STERN GEAR

PLUMBING

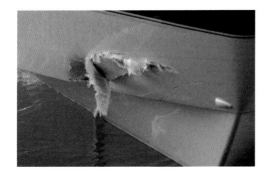

↖ *(far left) Collision damage to a hull has exposed the sandwich core inside.*

↑ *The securing bolts on this keel shoe need close examination.*

← *The attachment point of this deep bilge keel is showing signs of corrosion.*

unusual to see the attachment bolts that pass through the moulded hull work loose, which could allow water into the laminate. If the metal shoe extends aft to form the bottom support for the rudder, check that this extension hasn't bent in a grounding, which could strain the rudder bearings. There will almost certainly be corrosion in a metal shoe made from steel, so check whether the corrosion is just skin deep or more extensive – does it extend to the fastening bolts? A metal shoe is there to take the wear and tear, and it's quite easy to replace, but you want to be confident it's doing its job properly.

If and when you discover signs of grounding you may want to check the boat's history; it could well have been kept on a mooring at the harbour where it took the ground at low water, and any boat that has been at a grounding mooring will have been under additional stress, so look for signs of damage to the hull bottom, the rudders and propellers and of course the keel(s). Look for cracking or crazing in the gel coat of a composite hull, denting in a metal hull and wear in the planking and timbers of a wooden hull. Check sailboats with twin keels carefully for these signs. Other hulls that have taken the ground at a mooring may have the giveaway holes in the hull sides amidships where 'legs' have been attached to keep the boat upright when it takes the ground.

Checking composite hulls

FOR MANY OWNERS a composite hull is a mystery and potential owners go in fear of the dreaded osmosis (see below). The first thing to do when surveying a composite hull is to establish what the laminate consists of, so ask the broker, builder or take to the internet. It could be a solid laminate that has been built up with a hand lay-up system, during which each glass mat layer is placed manually into the hull and impregnated with the resin. Some modern types of lay-up use a similar system, but the resin is introduced under vacuum once the dry mat has been laid in the mould. A third system introduces a foam or balsa core into the laminate to create what is known as sandwich construction, and this might cover the whole of the hull structure or just parts, the rest being solid laminate. The hull may be stiffened with additional internal frames and stringers, which are added into the mould, or in a more modern system an internal lining is added, which is a separate moulding that fits inside the hull moulding and serves both to stiffen the

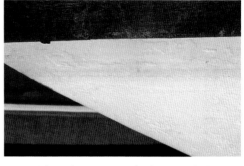

↑ *Apart from the waterline chip, this has the appearance of a problematic thick paint layer rather than a gel coating.*

↓ *This pitting looks as though it is only in the anti-fouling paint rather than the gel coat.*

hull moulding as well as introduce some of the internal divisions and structures of the yacht interior. If you can get this 'deep level' construction information, you'll have a much better chance of knowing what to look for.

→ *Osmosis bubbles in the gel coat.*

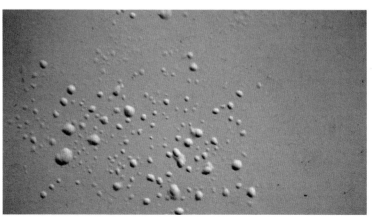

WHY SURVEY YOUR OWN BOAT?

THE TOOLS OF THE TRADE

THE HULL

DECK AND SUPERSTRUCTURE

ENGINES AND THEIR SYSTEMS

STERN GEAR

PLUMBING

OSMOSIS

Osmosis is mainly caused by water permeating the gel coat and creating bubbles between the laminate and the coating when it expands. It will usually present in a series of hard 'bubbles' on the surface of the gel coat. Small bubbles in localised areas don't pose a particularly serious problem, but they do need to be ground out and filled with resin and then smoothed down to restore the finish. You'll probably require a paint job to fully restore the topsides. Osmosis can also occur in the underwater surfaces that are constantly submerged; you should be able to detect gel coat bubbles by touch, unless there are several layers of antifouling paint that have built up, in which case you may want to scratch some off to investigate. More extensive areas of osmosis bubbles may require areas to be ground off and extensive re-coating with proprietary systems. For yachts that are perhaps less than five years old the risk from osmosis

↑ Osmosis being treated below the waterline on this hull.

↓ Osmosis bubbles being filled.

should be small because of advances in the materials and methods of construction, but it's still worth checking.

Osmosis bubbles may be small, so you'll need more than just a quick glance at the surface; go over the whole hull surface in detail, both looking and touching. Mark sections on the hull with your tape to be sure you don't miss a spot.

CHIPS, CRACKS AND SCRATCHES

While you're looking for bubbles, also check for scratches, chips and cracks in the gel coat. Scratches are often shallow and feathered and you may be able to feel their roughness rather than see it. They tend to be more of a cosmetic problem and can often be polished out. Of course, deeper scratches and/or chips that penetrate the laminate need more attention. Both deep scratches and chips should be ground out and filled with new gel coating, then smoothed down to prevent water entering the laminate.

Because cracks will normally extend down to the laminate under the gel coat they tend to fill with dirt, which can make them more visible. Cracks need to be taken more seriously because apart from possibly letting water into the laminate, they're usually a sign that the hull has been under some sort of stress. Those that radiate from a single point may indicate impact damage while longer cracks could indicate undue flexing of the hull, perhaps caused by coming alongside too hard.

Cracking of the gel coat can occur around fittings that have been under stress. If you find this kind of damage, you need to turn your attention to the inside of the hull because the impact or flexing that caused the cracks in the gel coat may have been serious enough to stress the internal stiffening of the hull, to the point that it can detach from the main hull moulding. Because this internal stiffening is normally added after completion of the main hull moulding, the bonding between hull and stiffening may be weak and any impact to or flexing of the hull moulding could cause the bond to break. You can see this defect fairly easily: if the edge of the stiffener is lifting away slightly from the hull moulding, the problem is serious. The stiffener won't be doing its job properly and may let water into the gap, which the foam former will absorb in turn, leading to further deterioration. Do as much as you can to examine the attachment of the internal hull stiffeners, although access to these internal areas is rarely possible without dismantling half of the interior.

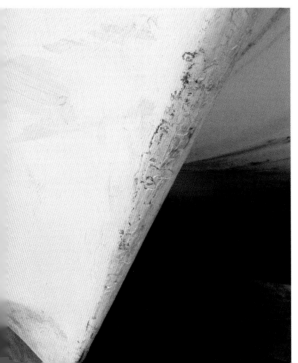

← The chip damage to the stem of this boat was probably caused by the anchor chain.

↑ These marks look like osmosis but they are probably just the remains of marine growth.

WHY SURVEY YOUR OWN BOAT?

THE TOOLS OF THE TRADE

THE HULL

DECK AND SUPERSTRUCTURE

ENGINES AND THEIR SYSTEMS

STERN GEAR

PLUMBING

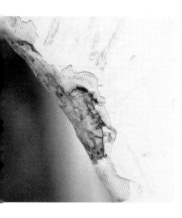

← Serious laminate damage in the stem.

→ Repair to slight bow damage is now ready for finishing off.

↓ This impact damage has been filled and sealed and is ready to rub down.

Often the stiffening takes the form of rigid plywood bulkheads that are bonded into the hull and these may create hard points where the slight flexing of the hull moulding comes into contact with the rigid bulkhead, which could lead to delamination. Do take the trouble to examine the attachment of the engine bearers in the engine compartment, which can be a high stress area – the base of the bearers at least should be accessible in most cases.

It is easy to examine the topsides of the hull for scratches, chips and cracks, since the gel coat is exposed, but below the waterline the hull will have been painted with antifouling so that cracks and other defects are not likely to show up so well. This is a dilemma for any surveyor, so it can pay to scrape off the antifouling in selected areas to check what is going on underneath, provided you have permission to do so. You would be justified in doing this if you had found problems in the topside examination that might extend below. Otherwise, selected areas might be at the turn of the bilge on a sailboat or at the chine on the motorboat. On planing motorboats you'll want to check along the sharp edges of the chines and spray rails because it can be difficult to lay up the laminate into these depressions so there may be voids that could show up later as chip-like marks in the gel coat. Composite structures in general do not take kindly to sharp edges and corners so that these can be the first areas to show signs of trouble. When there is no fendering, transom corners are especially vulnerable to chips and scratches.

In areas where you can't remove the antifouling paint below the waterline at least try to feel the surface. Look along the surface for any slight distortion that may indicate a past repair.

On planing motorboat hulls the laminate comes under considerable pressure when the boat is running at speed in waves. Obviously the hull laminate and structure should have been designed to cope with this and it is normal to see the hull skin supported by longitudinal stringers

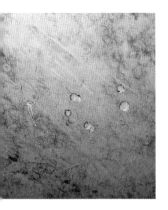

← It looks like the osmosis bubbles have been opened up.

which reduce the hard spots and reduce the chance of corrugations developing. However, there can be considerable flexing of the hull panels so look for cracking of the gel coat around those panels that join to stiffer areas, such as around the keel and the chines. Check also for signs of delamination in the frames and stringers, particularly around bulkhead edges. It's not unknown for a plywood bulkhead to crack horizontally if it can't accommodate the flexing. This especially would suggest that this planing boat has had a hard life and you'll want to take a closer look, and certainly if it has sandwich construction.

SANDWICH CONSTRUCTION

Sandwich construction hulls can pose particular problems for surveyors. There was a time when sandwich construction was in vogue, because it created a stiffer laminate that required less internal framing and added sound and heat insulation. However, having the inner and outer layers of laminate separated by a foam or end grain balsa layer a centimetre or two in thickness has been the cause of many failures.

The major problem with sandwich construction is that the bonding between the three layers can become detached due to flexing of the structure in a seaway, allowing water in. Sandwich construction relies on good bonding between the layers for its structural strength so if the bonding fails there is only the relatively thin outer layer keeping the water out and failure can occur. If the bonding fails, the three layers may be moving independently of one another which breaks up the middle softer layer of semi-rigid foam and tends to invite water into the gap. Water may enter through cracks in the laminate or poorly

← Damage to the stem has been filled on this hull and is ready for rubbing down and finishing.

↑ This chip in the transom edge has been filled.

WHY SURVEY YOUR OWN BOAT?

THE TOOLS OF THE TRADE

THE HULL

DECK AND SUPERSTRUCTURE

ENGINES AND THEIR SYSTEMS

STERN GEAR

PLUMBING

sealed fastenings in the hull, such as seacock inlets, chain plates or other hull fittings, and even if there is no water entry the overall strength of the laminate will be weakened.

You may find sandwich construction through the entire hull but it's more likely to be found in the topsides only, particularly on a planing motorboat where the pounding of the hull in waves at speed can be detrimental to sandwich construction if it starts to flex. Therefore, if you suspect sandwich construction in the hull you're surveying, try to establish which sections have solid and which have sandwich construction. You may have access to the hull specification but if you don't, use your hammer to 'tap it out'. The sandwich sections 'absorb' the sound, and you should be especially suspicious of a 'dull' sound,

since it could indicate delamination or the presence of water in the sandwich. Check fixtures and fittings in the area, but remember that these are usually made from solid laminate or plywood inserts in the sandwich.

In fact, your suspicions should be raised if you come across any sign of cracking or impact on the gel coat of a sandwich hull, as this could be a route for water to enter the laminate. If a boat (of either solid or sandwich construction) has been outside in the winter months and water has entered the laminate, there is a possibility that the trapped water will have frozen and expanded so that a gradual process of delamination occurs. If you suspect that a sandwich hull is not sound, it's probably wise to walk away from the purchase. If it is your own boat, you could use a moisture meter (see chapter 2) to assess the moisture levels in the hull, although these are tricky to operate. In this instance, I'd probably recommend calling in a surveyor for a professional diagnosis.

DEALING WITH PAINTED SURFACES

While owners tend to take great care of the outside of the hull the inside is much more likely to be left to its own devices. Look for lifting edges where the hull

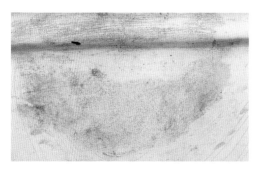

↑ *The cracks suggest that this is impact damage and will require close investigation inside and out.*

↓ *This is a cross section of a sandwich laminate where water has found its way between the outer skin and the core.*

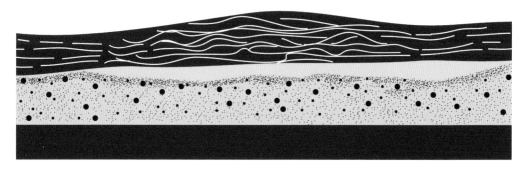

framing and stringers have been faired in and examine areas that have a fresh coat of paint, as this may have been applied to cover up a repair or damage. Poke around with your spike to ensure that everything is firmly attached, particularly around the engine beds and bulkheads where the stresses can be higher. There should be adequate access to all the skin fittings on the inside, so check carefully around the edges of these and the securing bolts for any signs of weeping, perhaps indicating a poor seal or water in the laminate.

On some older composite boats you may find that the hull, and at least the topsides, have been painted, which should ring alarm bells. It could be that the topsides needed a 'freshen up' but equally the paint could be covering restoration work, undertaken to cure osmosis or other topside damage. If the paint job was for cosmetic reasons, it's likely that the owner or broker will admit to this, otherwise you should delve a little deeper. A professional paint job may be hard to detect because it will look like the original gel coat, but you may be able to scrape away some of the antifouling to check the hull condition underneath. If you can see brush marks, indicating a poor paint job, you'll have a major job on your hands to restore the hull to a good finish, in which case I'd recommend you walk away.

WHY SURVEY YOUR OWN BOAT?

THE TOOLS OF THE TRADE

THE HULL

DECK AND SUPERSTRUCTURE

ENGINES AND THEIR SYSTEMS

STERN GEAR

PLUMBING

Composite hull

- [ ] Is the hull/keel joint secure on sailboats?
- [ ] Is the keel band secure on motorboats?
- [ ] Does the glass reinforcing show through?
- [ ] Are there hull blisters?
- [ ] Are there chips in the gel coat?
- [ ] Are there scratches in the gel coat?
- [ ] Are there spidery impact cracks in the gel coat?
- [ ] Are the topsides painted?
- [ ] Are there corner chips?
- [ ] Is there scuffing on the surface?
- [ ] Are there chips along the chine and spray rail edges on powerboats?

↓ The paint on this hull could hide defects.

Checking wooden hulls

WHEN SURVEYING a wooden hull you are looking for a range of ailments affecting the wood and the structure of the boat. What that is will be determined to a certain extent by the construction method used for the hull, the wood type and the finish on the timber. The most common construction system is planking laid up on the frames and timbers that give the hull its shape, and this is usually quite easy to identify because the seams between the planks will almost certainly show somewhere, unless the boat has had a very recent paint job. Wood is always on the move, expanding when wet and tending to contract as it dries out. This puts pressure on the caulking- or spline-sealed seams.

DRYING OUT: CAULKING AND SPLINES

Traditionally caulking was oakum hammered into the seam to seal it and then covered with tar or a proprietary caulking material. Wooden splines – finely tapered cross-section strips of wood hammered in to seal the gap – were less common. Both traditional systems are still used on many wooden fishing and work boats, but yacht builders tend to use either modern caulking compounds or splines, both of which allow a better finish to be retained on the topsides. Therefore, you're looking for any sign that the caulking is coming loose or is damaged. You want to look carefully around the stem and the stern where the planking ends are sealed to the timbers because this is where you're most likely

to detect any movement or shrinking that could dislodge the caulking. The planking at the bow is under stress because it was bent in a curve to generate the right shape, and it is the fastenings at the stem or stern that hold the planking in place. If you do find that caulking has dislodged it may be possible to hammer it back into position, but the timbers may have been allowed to dry out, thus widening the gap. If drying out has been the cause you may see some longitudinal splits in the timbers at the bow and stern because these timbers will often slip when drying out. Unless it looks serious this should not be a major problem because the wood will swell back to its original shape when it gets wet again, but serious drying out can distort the timbers and planking beyond any hope of restoration.

↓ *This paint peeling suggests that there is a problem inside the hull that should be checked.*

↓ *This wooden hull has been allowed to dry out, which has caused the seams to open up.*

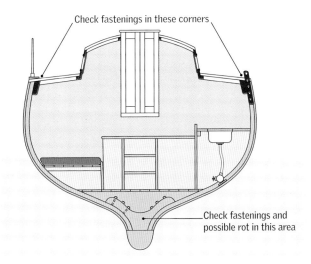

Check fastenings in these corners

Check fastenings and possible rot in this area

↑ *This is a cross section of a wooden hull showing how the timbers are linked.*

→ *The planking seams are visible on this wooden hull but this is only a cosmetic problem.*

If planking has warped (curved across the grain), it can signal drying out or poor quality wood. Warping places a strain on both the fastening and seams, so look for signs of corrosion – a green coloured stain if the fastenings are copper or rust stains if they are steel. The galvanised fastenings often used on fishing boats can have a characteristic whitish stain, a result of the reaction between the zinc and the acidity of the wood. You'll find this mainly around bolts used to connect hull timbers and framing, since acidic oak is often used here. Small amounts close to the fastening may not be serious but if it has become more extensive it can soften the wood so that the whole structure becomes weakened.

As a minimum step the fastening should be withdrawn for examination and this should reveal not only any corrosion but also the extent of the soft timber. Poke around with your spike or bradawl to reveal the state of the timber without dismantling.

You don't want to be sticking the sharp point of your pricker into the pristine finish of the topsides, but if you see any signs of rot or damage you may want to explore further. A slight wrinkling or split in the paint finish usually signals some sort of disturbance underneath, so give it a gentle tap with your hammer; a sound wooden hull should have a nice clear 'ring' when tapped, so start exploring further if you don't get this response.

WHY SURVEY YOUR OWN BOAT?

THE TOOLS OF THE TRADE

THE HULL

DECK AND SUPERSTRUCTURE

ENGINES AND THEIR SYSTEMS

STERN GEAR

PLUMBING

39

↑ *The state of this hull looks bad but it may only need the seams re-caulking and repainting.*

↑ *There is a small indication of movement between the planking and the transom here.*

the grain, and it is extremely difficult to cure short of stripping out the infected wood. I recommend you walk away from any wooden yacht infected with dry rot. If you already own the boat, you need to deal with dry rot head on, so contact a professional surveyor.

Wet rot, as its name suggests, is caused when timbers are constantly wet and don't

← *A doubler has been fitted alongside a frame that has cracked.*

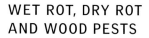

↓ *Severe chafe on this plywood hull.*

WET ROT, DRY ROT AND WOOD PESTS

Inside the hull you should have much more freedom to explore with your spike, which is good because this is where you're likely to find trouble on a wooden hull. Before you start pricking the timbers, sniff the air: both wet and dry rot have their characteristic smells, dry rot tending to smell 'dry' because it is a form of fungus while wet rot has a damper smell to it. Dry rot is also usually visible in the white cobweb-like fungus that spreads across and into the wood and by cracking across

receive adequate ventilation, the sort of conditions that often exist inside a boat. If it lies under a painted surface you'll see it in the cracking and splitting of the painted surface. Unfinished wood tends to show cracks across the grain and the wood has a sponge-like texture. For wet rot to form it usually needs a combination of damp and stale air so if you can change the atmosphere in the area, you can possibly dry out the contaminated area and treat it with wood preservative if it affects only a small region. Larger areas and rot in frames and timbers may require replacement or doubling timbers, so seek expert advice. Once cured, wet rot should not return if adequate ventilation of the area is put in place. However, I would hesitate to go ahead with the purchase of a boat where wet rot has been detected unless you can be sure of its extent and are prepared to carry out the required restoration work.

Now we come to the bugs that like to chew wood. Woodworm – the same type found in a house – is the most common,

although it is less likely to infect boats because it prefers dry wood and the harder woods used in boat building are less prone to infection. However, it can infect the internal fittings and fixtures. Woodworm is detected by tiny holes and a timber coloured dust on the surface, which is the residue left by the worms as they bore their way into the wood. Once established, you can cure woodworm with proprietary solutions but you need to be certain you have detected all the woodworm-infected areas on board.

More serious among timber boring pests is the gribble, a larger creature that bores a hole perhaps 2 or 3mm in diameter. A gribble worm bores along the grain and doesn't usually come to the surface until it has damaged much of the interior of the wood, so it can seriously weaken a timber without there being much external evidence besides the entry holes. If water gets into the bore holes it can start wet rot, which may be the first signs of a gribble worm problem, but also check areas where

← *The way the cracks have opened up in these hull timbers would be a cause for concern.*

↑ *The gaps around the plank in the middle might indicate that the fastenings are not secure.*

WHY SURVEY YOUR OWN BOAT?

THE TOOLS OF THE TRADE

THE HULL

DECK AND SUPERSTRUCTURE

ENGINES AND THEIR SYSTEMS

STERN GEAR

PLUMBING

41

↑ *The corrosion showing through the paintwork suggests that either the fitting inside or the fastenings are deteriorating.*

you can see the end grain of the wood, such as inside a hole cut for a seacock; modern antifouling paints have had an impact on gribble but any areas such as this where the paint does not reach can provide the entry point. A soft hammer tap sound could indicate trouble that would demand a closer inspection by an expert.

Signs of rot and worm in a timber hull may not always be apparent from the outside so you need to get as much access to the interior as possible. Interior access on wooden hulls is usually easier than with composite hulls as they tend to be one-off buildings without complex interior linings. The obvious place to start your interior inspection is in the bilges where water may lie or may have been lying. Unless it is a very smart construction you shouldn't have a problem poking around with your pricker in these interior timbers. Look carefully at

points where the frames and timbers meet the planking, places where water might have been trapped and the rotting process has started. If the wood has been left bare, you might be able to identify the problem areas by discolouration of the wood, and certainly any discolouration should be examined closely. It might just be an oil stain or possibly an area where water has been lying in the past, but it's better to be safe than sorry. While you are doing this internal examination also check any visible fastenings in the same way. It can be a good idea to draw some of the fastenings if you do see or hear signs of trouble, otherwise they are best left alone.

OTHER TYPES OF WOODEN CONSTRUCTION

Plywood has been widely used in boat building both for hull construction and internal partitions and panelling. Good quality marine plywood is a very durable material that isn't likely to be prone to rot or worm unless there are exposed edges. These exposed edges can absorb water and if that water should freeze, it can start to force the layers of wood in the plywood apart, which could start the rotting process. In general, take the same approach for checking a plywood hull as you would a timber and frame hull.

If the hull is constructed from plywood panels, you need to check it for any signs of rippling in the surface and along the edges, which can indicate delamination. The likely construction method would see the plywood panels attached to the hull with both glue and screws or bolts. If screws have been used, any movement in the hull might pull these screws, so any screw heads standing proud should be a cause for concern.

Cold moulded hull construction should be very durable because in many ways it is similar to a laminate hull. In cold moulded construction the glass of the laminate is replaced by thin strips of wood that are laid up in the desired shape and secured with stainless steel staples and epoxy glues. Once the epoxy has cured, the wood should be fully sealed against water ingress. Look for signs of discolouration, which would indicate that water has got into the wood. There may also be areas of wet rot in some of the internal timbers where water has been lying in contact with the wood.

Checking metal hulls

STEEL HULLS

Let's look at steel hulls first because they tend to be more common than aluminium. When corrosion is present in steel there is a very obvious giveaway sign and that is rust. If there is rust on the steel, it will fight its way through any paint finish to the surface quite quickly, certainly before the corrosion gets to the point where it can be serious. During a survey, therefore, you're on the look out for the very distinctive signs of rust, which are very obvious on a

WHY SURVEY YOUR OWN BOAT?

THE TOOLS OF THE TRADE

THE HULL

DECK AND SUPERSTRUCTURE

ENGINES AND THEIR SYSTEMS

STERN GEAR

PLUMBING

Wooden hulls

SURVEY CHECKLIST

☐ Is the hull/keel joint on sailboats free of a gap or discolouration?
☐ Is the keel band intact on motorboats?
☐ Are the plank seams pronounced?
☐ Is the caulking intact?
☐ Is the paint finish intact?
☐ Is the paint finish along the grain free of cracking?
☐ Are the stem and surrounding timbers free of slits?
☐ Is the transom intact?
☐ Are the plank ends at the transom secure?
☐ Have you checked for signs of soft wood indicating wet rot?
☐ Is the boat free of the musty smell of dry rot?
☐ Are the plank fastenings free of signs of discolouration?

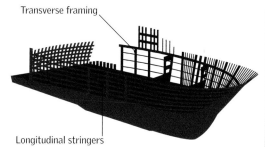

Transverse framing

Longitudinal stringers

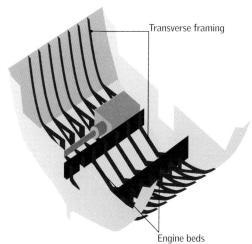

Transverse framing

Engine beds

↑ *The type of hull framing that you might find on a steel hull.*

↑ *In this hull the light steel framing needs a close examination because of the thin steel.*

light coloured hull. The most obvious places to look are on the welded seams of the hull, which tend to provide a good source of rust potential because the welding has been laid down under intense heat. Access to the interior is important: you're much more likely to find rust here, along the welding that links the frames with the hull plating, and a damp atmosphere can create the breeding ground for rust to form.

Having found signs of rust the next step is to determine how serious it is. Light rust on the surface of the steel isn't usually a problem, provided that the rust is removed and the area properly painted. What you are looking for here are the signs of deeper pockets of rust, that which is serious enough to have eroded the surface of the steel and reduced the thickness of plating or frames. Strangely enough the evidence of this deeper form of corrosion is likely to be shown by a rise in the steel surface. This is because when steel is

converted into rust, which is a form of iron oxide, it absorbs oxygen and this increases the volume of the rust compared with that of the original steel. In terms of its thickness then, a patch of rust may look very threatening if you assumed that the amount of rust was equal to the amount of steel that had been eroded away, but in fact the volume of rust will be something in the order of ten times the amount of fixed steel. This doesn't mean you should ignore it, because rust is always going to get worse; the slightly porous nature of rust means that it can hold water even when the surrounding area is dry.

You'll also want to find out what has caused the rust in the first place. Perhaps it was water dripping from above, a poor paint job that hasn't effectively sealed the

→ This corrosion is probably only caused by abrasion and is little more than skin deep.

surface or an impurity in the original steel that has set up a little galvanic cell. Modern steel hulls have usually been sandblasted after construction and painted with epoxy paints, which provide excellent corrosion protection but even with such a hull you want to check the surface for scratches or scrapes that may have damaged the coating. These will need treating before

the rust gets in and starts its nasty work. I have come across small areas of steel where corrosion has started for no apparent reason and it has eroded away perhaps half the thickness of the steel in a very local area. This could come from an impurity in the steel or it might be down to something as minor as a coin being dropped into the bilge, the two dissimilar metals reacting in the presence of water.

Whenever you find corrosion both inside and outside the hull you must chip away the rust to find out the extent of the corrosion. Get permission from the owner or broker

↑ Well-maintained steel work inside a riveted steel hull.

↑ This steel hull has had a thick layer of filler applied to fair the hull shape.

WHY SURVEY YOUR OWN BOAT?

THE TOOLS OF THE TRADE

THE HULL

DECK AND SUPERSTRUCTURE

ENGINES AND THEIR SYSTEMS

STERN GEAR

PLUMBING

45

before you do this because not everybody likes having their lovely steel hull chipped away, but you do need to find out how much of the steel has been eroded away. On a yacht the steel plating might be quite thin, perhaps just 4–6mm, so any reduction in this thickness through corrosion could impact upon the integrity of the hull. It can be quite easy to repair corroded areas by cutting out the affected portions and welding in a new piece, but it does mean getting access both inside and out.

As with a composite hull you need to go over every inch of the hull as far as possible because corrosion can be very localised. If you find the corrosion is extensive, it's probably a good idea to walk away from the boat. However, fishing and workboats with heavy scantlings can still function with quite extensive corrosion, as long as it is not deep pitting. Sharp edges and corners will be most prone to this type of damage. When you find rust spots and have chipped out the rust down to the hard steel below hold a straight edge across the area to see how deep the pitting is; anything over a quarter of the thickness of the plate should be cause for concern.

Of course, you'll also want to check a steel hull for any damage or distortion that may have been caused by collision. Allowing for the distortion that welding can create, a modern steel yacht hull should still come out relatively fair and smooth.

ALUMINIUM HULLS

Aluminium boats are actually quite rare these days and along with it being a difficult material to survey adequately, the chances of getting involved with aluminium are slim. However, there may be aluminium fittings on other boats so it pays to have some knowledge of its qualities.

Unlike steel hulls, you won't find rust on an aluminium hull. However, you're more likely to find corrosion of a different type: electrolysis. This is caused when two dissimilar metals are connected, setting up what is in effect a battery between them, which leads to corrosion. Being the 'lighter' metal, aluminium is usually the one that suffers. Builders of aluminium boats should take care to prevent contact between different metals by insulating them, but over time the insulation may have broken down. You can also get corrosion resulting from action between a bronze propeller or bronze skin fittings, but anodes, which are made of an even lighter metal than aluminium, should take care of that. Sailboats with an aluminium hull and an iron keel are also cause for concern, but again they should be insulated or at least anode protected.

Steel hulls

SURVEY CHECKLIST

- ☐ Is the outside surface free of corrosion?
- ☐ Is the inside surface free of corrosion?
- ☐ What is the type of corrosion?
- ☐ What is the depth of pitting?
- ☐ Is the hull free of evidence of dents/a collision?
- ☐ Is the construction of a high quality?
- ☐ Is the paint job of a high quality?

WHY SURVEY YOUR OWN BOAT?

THE TOOLS OF THE TRADE

THE HULL

DECK AND SUPERSTRUCTURE

ENGINES AND THEIR SYSTEMS

STERN GEAR

PLUMBING

Aluminium hulls

- ☐ Is the hull (both inside and out) free of corrosion?
- ☐ Is the hull free of electrolytic pitting?
- ☐ Are the anodes in good condition?
- ☐ Are the joints between dissimilar metals in good condition?
- ☐ Is the hull free of evidence of dents/a collision?
- ☐ Is the construction of a high quality?
- ☐ Is the paint job of a high quality?

Therefore, if you're surveying an aluminium boat you'll need to examine the hull both inside and out for the tell-tale white corrosion powder which shows that all is not well. Broken wires, later additions of metal fittings, even the wrong type of antifouling paint can cause problems on an aluminium hull, so if you find corrosion, you'll need to call in a specialist to determine the cause.

Some boats combine a steel or composite hull with an aluminium superstructure. Composite and aluminium are quite compatible, but steel and aluminium have to be carefully insulated from each other to survive. Check the insulation carefully where possible.

STAINLESS STEEL

Stainless steel is a steel alloy with a minimum of 10.5 per cent chromium content by mass. The stainless normally used in the marine environment is 316, which works pretty well as far as combining strength, corrosion resistance and shaping abilities. However, 316 stainless is also more expensive, so you can find cheaper alternatives, and there are a large number of these, and there is no easy way to assess which type has been used.

Even high quality stainless steel can be subject to rust streaks if a tiny bit of the steel is exposed, and you are much more likely to get these when the stainless has a matte or a machined surface, i.e. on the threads of a rigging screw. You are far less likely to see rust streaks on highly polished stainless, such as handrails and some other fittings. Besides, you don't need to be too concerned about rust streaks on stainless steel as it's unlikely to be anything more than skin deep, so it should just be a matter of polishing it off.

All hull inspections take time and patience and you need to have all your senses on high alert, because the clues to any potential issues can often be quite small and easily bypassed, especially since it is not unknown for sellers to temporarily cover them up. Buying a yacht can be an emotional business and it's easy to convince yourself that any problems are not serious, but hull problems are generally the hardest or most expensive to cure. Keep reminding yourself that the hull is the only thing between you and the water; you don't want to take any chances with your life.

4 DECK AND SUPER STRUCTURE

↑ *Window frames in the superstructure need close examination.*

↑ *Impact damage to the rubbing strip on the transom corner.*

WHILE MUCH OF the survey tends to be focused on the hull because of its critical role in keeping the boat afloat, the superstructure has an arguably equally important role and needs careful assessment. Many of the techniques used for surveying the hull apply to surveying the deck and superstructure.

On a composite boat you are likely to find more areas with a foam core in the deck and superstructure, while the framing on metal and wooden boats is likely to be lighter but more complex because of the different shapes it has to accommodate. You'll also need to consider windows and a multitude of other fixtures and fittings.

The entire deck and superstructure area should be self-draining, either through washing over the side or scuppers and drains, and water should not be able to collect in any area. That is the theory, but in practice you are likely to find that water can collect, perhaps just inside the toe rail amidships or in cockpit areas, depending on the angle of the boat when it is stored ashore. Even if they are dry during the survey, you can usually detect water collection areas by staining on the deck and it pays to look at such areas a bit more closely. Any water almost permanently on deck can start corrosion on a steel hull or rot on a wooden boat, or it could permeate through cracks in the gel coat on a composite boat.

Gaining access

WHILE THE INTERIOR of the hull on both power and sailboats is usually reasonably accessible, designers tend to overlook this when it comes to the inside of the superstructure and fit linings. You may be able to get some sort of access by removing lights and other fittings, but it may be difficult to get to the likely problem areas in the corners and angles of the

WHY SURVEY YOUR OWN BOAT?

THE TOOLS OF THE TRADE

THE HULL

DECK AND SUPERSTRUCTURE

ENGINES AND THEIR SYSTEMS

STERN GEAR

PLUMBING

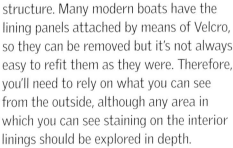

← *The complex fittings around the bow on sailboats need close examination.*

↑ *The cracking and corrosion around this vent suggest that it should be removed for inspection.*

used in addition to decorative linings. One ray of hope can come when the interior lining is attached in panels, which allows them to be easily pulled off and then re-attached. However if it's not your boat, you'll need permission to do this and then you'll need to take great care not to damage the panels and return them to the right spot (number the panels or make a note of where each one is located). Even when you can get access in this way you may well find that you come across insulation, and on metal structures this may take the form of sprayed-on rigid foam which is virtually impossible to remove; if you do remove it, it will need to be sprayed on again. Therefore, all you can really do is check for cracks or broken areas, which could indicate undue movement of the structure hidden behind.

ELECTROLYSIS

You need to be extra vigilant when examining the deck and superstructure on aluminium boats. Electrolysis could be a problem, particularly in areas of the

structure. Many modern boats have the lining panels attached by means of Velcro, so they can be removed but it's not always easy to refit them as they were. Therefore, you'll need to rely on what you can see from the outside, although any area in which you can see staining on the interior linings should be explored in depth.

A lot will depend on how the superstructure and deck have been constructed and, as always, older boats tend to have better access than modern ones where interior mouldings are often

WHY SURVEY YOUR OWN BOAT?

THE TOOLS OF THE TRADE

THE HULL

DECK AND SUPERSTRUCTURE

ENGINES AND THEIR SYSTEMS

STERN GEAR

PLUMBING

↑ *This mast came down as a result of the stem head fitting and deck giving way.*

superstructure where no anodes are fitted. Stainless steel and aluminium are reasonably compatible and their proximity should not cause major problems but if aluminium is in contact with normal steel, copper, brass and bronze and the area gets a regular soaking of sea water you could be facing significant corrosion, and the aluminium is always the one to suffer. The boat builder would hopefully have addressed this potential problem, but additions to the boat may not have been subject to the same scrutiny and could start a reaction. Check deck fittings for a white powder or crystalline substance, which could signal aluminium electrolytic corrosion. If you do discover it, there are solutions; you could insulate the two metals, although securing bolts are very difficult to insulate so, even better, replace the offending metal fixture with one made from a more compatible material.

Areas of stress

THE DECK AND superstructure of a sailboat is a high stress area of the boat; on sailboats, the mast, winches, stanchions supporting the rails are all attached to the deck, and all of these can generate heavy local loads. On motorboats, the windlass in the bow and the various mooring fittings, capstans, stanchions and davits can generate load, while even people walking about on the deck may create stress. Therefore, designers have to create

↓ *There has been considerable impact damage in this bow area.*

51

a structure that can handle all of these stresses without too much distortion.

One of the quickest ways to check the structural integrity of the deck and superstructure is to walk around the deck, cockpit and coachroof and try bouncing; the structures should be rigid enough to take this sort of loading, so if you detect movement under your feet it's time to investigate. It might be that the structure is simply not as strong as it could be, but you won't want to let it go unchecked. On a composite boat, movement could indicate that the bond between the laminates of a sandwich moulding is breaking apart and has lost some of its rigidity. On metal and wooden boats, there could be inadequate framing or support for the deck or coachroof structure, while any movement is likely to open up gaps which could lead to nasty leaks.

↑ Careless handling has probably caused these deep chips on the transom corner.

↓ A new section of rubbing rail has been used to cover up partially the superstructure moulding behind it.

Panelling and decks: sharp edges, joins and corners

PANELLING

EXAMINE THE INTERIOR for signs of leaks in the joins around the edges of the panelling on wood and metal boats, while on a composite look for gel coat cracks around the edges of the flexing panels. Light tapping with a hammer might indicate a problem in a laminate; the sound will change from a ring to a softer thud, although you'll have to take into account that rigidity changes across the panel structure and hard points vary (making it much harder to get meaningful information using this method than it is when examining the hull).

On a motorboat you may find some movement in the large panel areas of the flybridge deck or the superstructure top. These can be quite large unsupported areas because the designers want a clear space below, but the structure also has to be rigid enough to support the large areas of glass that are often incorporated into the superstructure side panel.

Pay particular attention to the edges and corners of mouldings and structures. This is where you're most likely to find problems, since these can be the focus of stress. Composite mouldings in particular do not like sharp edges and corners because, on the one hand, it can be harder for the laminator to get the glass mat and the resin into these corners while on the other, composite mouldings tend to rely on a smooth transition around bends and corners for strength. A panel with a double curve is a lot more rigid than a flat panel because it has less scope for flexing.

↓ A clear point of impact damage that is highlighted by dirt getting into the cracks.

You're most likely to find sharp edges and corners in the cockpit and coachroof on a sailboat and around the superstructure on a motorboat. Check for any cracking in the gel coat, which could indicate undue stress. It may not be a major problem and the gel coat can be ground out and replaced, but the problem won't go away without a change in the shape of the moulding. Moreover, it reflects bad design in general, meaning you may want to walk away now.

On a wooden boat, sharp corners and edges are more acceptable because the material is structured that way and will only bend in one direction, but look closely for any signs of movement at the edges which could indicate that the structure is not rigid enough. Such movement would also allow water to enter the small gaps, which could of course set off rot.

DECKS AND TRIM

Wooden boat decks and coachroofs are large flat areas, hence they are often constructed from large plywood panes. Here you need to look closely at where they attach to the rest of the structure; you're looking for signs of wrinkling or small undulations in the surface that could indicate water has got into the joint and started to cause delamination. While the signs may be small, the problem is a big one because you'll usually need to replace the entire panel. You may find that a fillet with a rounded edge has been added to the joint at the corners of the coachroof in order to help smooth the transition between two panels (one nearly horizontal and one nearly vertical), and such joints are prone to letting water in if there has been any small movement in the structure.

The decks of older wooden boats may be constructed from wooden strips laid over the supporting timbers, much in the same way that a hull is planked. As with the hull, the planks depend on good sealing of the joints for water tightness so you need to look closely at the seams to ensure that the caulking and the sealer or pitch over it remains intact. Any signs of leaking are usually evident below in the form of staining on the lining or paintwork. Bear

WHY SURVEY YOUR OWN BOAT?

THE TOOLS OF THE TRADE

THE HULL

DECK AND SUPERSTRUCTURE

ENGINES AND THEIR SYSTEMS

STERN GEAR

PLUMBING

← The sad looking state of this coachroof demands closer inspection.

in mind that the water may have tracked along the seam before it finds its way out in the form of a leak, so you'll need to search for its source.

Metal structures will almost always have sharp edges and corners because this is the way that the structure is put together when welded. These hard edges are often softened with wood trim to improve the appearance, so you'll need to look closely at the join between wood and

↓ The sealer in the seams on this wooden deck has deteriorated possibly causing leaks below.

metal to detect whether or not water has entered and started rot in the wood or corrosion in the metal. In fact, problems often present where two materials have been used in the construction of the deck and superstructure, since they can have different rates of expansion and contraction and/or reactions to slight flexing of the structure, all of which can open up small gaps, allowing water in to do its worst. Trouble like this is likely to be most evident around the securing points.

Composite boats may also include a wooden trim, so be sure to examine the join between a wooden rubbing strip and the moulding underneath. The join was probably filled with sealer when new, which may have since hardened or even dropped out; the gap can hold water and start to rot the wood.

You can get the same problem in window frame trims and indeed anywhere in the joins between the wood and mouldings. Green moss in the join is always a giveaway, but it isn't necessarily a serious problem because the wood can quite easily be replaced or even just the seam raked out and resealed. It could be more serious on a steel hull, since there could be deeper corrosion (look for rust streaks).

Teak decking or a substitute material improves the look of the boat and makes for a good anti-skid surface, but if the deck is strips of wood look carefully at the seams and edges for signs of water ingress. On a composite moulding, water getting in via these seams may not be a particularly serious problem except that it could eventually cause the wood and the moulding to separate, but this could cause corrosion on a steel structure. The teak used for decking is usually very durable and resistant to rot; however, today there are several substitute materials in use which have the look of teak but are applied in cut sheets. Provided there are no lifting edges and the sheets don't move when walked on or have a hollow sound when tapped, all should be well. If such wear is found, it will need re-gluing at the very least.

↑ *The sealing strip in this window corner has shrunk.*

↓ *Rubber window sealing can deteriorate through the influence of UV light.*

Windows, doors and hatches

WINDOWS

Windows should always be considered a potential source of trouble. The windows on earlier boats were set in frames, either wood or metal, and over time the seals would deteriorate and start to let water in. This will show in staining, usually around the bottom of the frame. You would almost

↑ *This window frame is slightly bowed suggesting water has got behind it*

WHY SURVEY YOUR OWN BOAT?

THE TOOLS OF THE TRADE

THE HULL

DECK AND SUPERSTRUCTURE

ENGINES AND THEIR SYSTEMS

STERN GEAR

PLUMBING

expect to find this on windows that open, and short of replacing the entire window there's probably not a lot you can do about it. On fixed windows you'll often see evidence of an application of new sealant; this should be a concern because it can be notoriously difficult to seal windows adequately once they start to leak. The only real solution is to take the window out and start from scratch to seal it back in place. You may also find these issues on older motorboat windscreens (the modern technique, similar to that used on cars, is to glue the glass panels into place).

Most composite modern boats include windows that are sealed directly against the composite moulding. Here the sealant also acts as a glue to hold the window in place, just as modern car windows are glued to the steel structure. This method appears to be very durable and you may find the glue/sealant backed up with screws or bolts to hold plastic (Lexan) windows securely in place, particularly those set into the hull topsides on a sailboat. Hull windows were very definitely frowned upon in the past because of the difficulties involved in adequately securing and sealing them, but modern motorboats not only have hull windows, they can be quite large in size. Many of these have become 'picture' windows that form part of the design styling and they need surveying with particular care because they can face considerable stress. Excepting small apertures, sailboat designers have largely resisted this trend, with windows confined mainly to the sides of the superstructure. Leaking in both hull and superstructure windows can be caused by flexing of the structure and all windows should be examined for any signs of deterioration in both the sealing and securing.

In addition to large hull windows, motorboats have increasing amounts of glass in the superstructure in order to create a light and airy interior, but the modern sealed and glued-in windows have a good track record so far provided that they are fitted into a suitably rigid

↓ Windows in the side of the hull need very careful scrutiny.

↓ This window seal may be intact, but a hose test might be a good idea.

structure. The glass itself should be fairly resistant to scratching and crazing, but you may find evidence of this on the earlier plastic windows. Although it doesn't look pretty, it rarely seriously weakens the window.

DOORS

Doors in the superstructure can be another source of trouble for much the same reasons. Traditionally wooden doors have been used to give a welcoming look to the boat, but they are rarely fully waterproof. Sealing methods transferred from the vehicle industry have made the doors on modern boats much more weather- and watertight, which is a great safety feature. Apart from checking that doors open and close easily, examine all around the seals to ensure the door is adequately bedded and free of damage which could cause leaks.

On sailboats traditional access to the interior is through an opening that can be fully or partially closed by shaped plywood boards. The object here is to be able to leave part of the opening open for ventilation and access but to prevent solid water finding its way below. Check that the boards are sound and well fitted.

HATCHES

Hatches are widely used on both motor- and sailboats to provide an alternative escape route from below in the event of fire and to allow sails to be shoved below during a sail change. Since they are let directly into the deck, are subject to solid water and have a low profile to prevent the crew tripping over them, they can have a hard life. Since a hatch is normally hinged at one end and clamped down at the other it's not always easy to get an even seal all round the hatch edge, so check the seal carefully. There may be some adjustment in the hinges on good quality hatches which can help you to even up the pressure on the seal. To really check watertightness, carry out a hose test (you could also do this for windows and doors). Any leakage through hatch seals is usually evident in staining or lining distortion in the vicinity of the opening.

Motorboats usually have hatches that give access to the engine compartment and on smaller boats these are often hinged flap hatches which open from the centreline outwards. It's difficult to get a good seal here, but since they are at the stern they are less subject to solid water. If they do leak, you are likely to see signs of corrosion on the engine fittings below or possibly stains in the bilges where the water has dripped down. Again, examine the seal for continuity and damage and mark it for renewal if necessary. Finally, check the closing arrangement to ensure it is closing and locking properly.

Many modern motorboats usually have the engine compartment access as a hatch let into the cockpit deck. It's a convenient arrangement as far as using the boat is concerned but the hatch has to be well sealed if it is to prevent water getting below in rough seas, rain or when washing down. The usual arrangement is to have the seal let into the hatch itself, so that it doesn't get damaged as crew go below, and then a channel is let in around the edge of the hatch opening, which is fitted with drains to drain off any standing water. The system works wonderfully well when the boat is new but damaged or worn seals and/or blocked drains can lead to leakage

WHY SURVEY YOUR OWN BOAT?

THE TOOLS OF THE TRADE

THE HULL

DECK AND SUPERSTRUCTURE

ENGINES AND THEIR SYSTEMS

STERN GEAR

PLUMBING

and you will see evidence of this in staining or corrosion below. I have seen boats in which electrical circuits, such as battery chargers, are installed on a bulkhead just below the hatch edge and even when the hatch is sealing properly, these can be vulnerable if the hatch has to be opened at sea or when it is raining. If you see such a set-up on your survey, carefully examine the connections and installations of the electrical system. You can check that the drains are clear with a hose test, but do this with care as you obviously want to avoid spraying water around the engine compartment.

Cockpit

THE COCKPIT ON a sailboat needs careful scrutiny because it can hold any water that might come on board in the form of spray or rain. The drains in the cockpit corners that remove any water are a vital safety feature, and they're a

↑ Check the bottom corners of the cockpit moulding carefully.

great place for muck, rope ends and debris to collect. Therefore, they must be clear and should be fitted with grids. Moreover, crew standing on the sole of the cockpit can cause flexing of the panels so be alert to any signs of the gel coat cracking on composite boats or rot or corrosion on wood and steel boats. Finally, check around those drain holes because if the drain is not fully sealed, water may find its way into the wood or laminate.

Fixtures and fittings

ALL OF THE fittings around the deck should come in for careful scrutiny. As we have already discussed, these can be subject to considerable stress. Therefore you are looking for any signs of movement or undue stress. On a composite these are revealed in cracking and/or crazing in the

↓ The sharp edges of the cockpit moulding could be a high stress area.

gel around the fitting, signs of wear in the wood surface on a wood boat and a sort of cocoa-looking powder on a steel boat. The latter is a form of rust that is created by movement between the two surfaces when there is a very slight slackness. In more extreme cases in both steel and aluminium hulls there could be distortion of the metal, while milder cases of stress or movement in the fitting will probably be revealed by a shiny surface on the aluminium where the parts rub together.

The problem may be caused by slackness in the fastenings of the fixture, in which case it can be hardened up. However, it would be better to remove the fitting and re-bed it in sealer, then harden up the securing bolts. Check the bolts too – if the

fitting has come loose they may need lock washers or nuts to prevent a recurrence. In any case, wherever there is slack or slight movement in a fitting take a closer look inside (if you can get access) to ensure there is adequate reinforcement to support the fitting. Doubling plates or internal wood pads in the moulding should always back up the securing bolts for high stress items on deck, such as block attachment points or winches.

GUARD RAIL STANCHIONS

One type of fixture that always seems to be under stress, particularly on sailboats where the crew work on deck, is the guard rail stanchions. People grab them when boarding from the dinghy or a low pontoon and hold on to them when moving about the deck at sea. It all adds up to heavy stress in the stanchion, which tends to be attached to the deck with just a small plate and two or three bolts. The leverage on the stanchion is high and on a composite deck it's not unusual to find stress cracks around its base. As this lies in the deck edge where water can collect there's a good chance of

↑ Many fairleads have sharp edges that can chafe a mooring rope.

↓ The cracking at the base of this pulpit stanchion indicates a stress area.

↓ The gel coat cracks show that this stanchion mounting has come under stress.

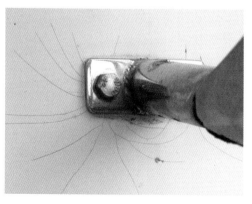

WHY SURVEY YOUR OWN BOAT?

THE TOOLS OF THE TRADE

THE HULL

DECK AND SUPERSTRUCTURE

ENGINES AND THEIR SYSTEMS

STERN GEAR

PLUMBING

water permeating into the laminate below the gel coat. If this water then freezes in winter, delamination can start to occur. If you find such cracks, the only solution is to remove the stanchion base, grind out the gel coat and renew it, then replace the stanchion, perhaps with a wider backing plate underneath to help spread the load. On boats with a laid wooden teak deck an indication of any movement in the stanchion base might be indicated by splitting in the teak and possibly slight lifting.

On some sailboats the stanchion is bolted to a metal toe rail which is then bolted to the deck edge. This arrangement helps to spread the load, but check the fastening area of the toe rail because the stress leverage on the stanchion is still present. On wooden boats you'll be looking at whether the securing bolts have moved and if there is any sign of stress in the backing plate below. It may be possible to just harden up the bolts to re-secure the stanchion. There shouldn't be a problem on steel boats, since the stanchions are likely to give way before the metal deck, although you may find some distortion in the deck plating on an aluminium boat if the plate is relatively thin.

Older motorboats may be fitted with the wire and stanchion method of guard rails, so you'll need to check these in the same way. The more modern method is to use tubular stainless steel for both the stanchions and the rails themselves, which creates a much more rigid structure that spreads the load and reduces stress at the deck attachment points. The pushpits and pulpits on sailboats are often constructed from stainless steel tubing, which usually stands quite a lot of stress and strain since these are integral structures that are intrinsically stiff, but check the deck mountings just to be sure.

DRAINAGE
Where bulwarks are fitted, usually on work and fishing boats, there has to be some means of draining water from the deck. The usual method is to have scuppers let into the lower sections and these may be fitted with hinged flaps that only open when there is water on the deck but stay closed to stop water coming on board. Check the hinges to ensure the flaps are free to move because large amounts of water on deck can lead to instability. Deck drains may be fitted to take water away from some areas, such as the cockpit on a sailboat or similar areas on a motorboat. These tend to exit below the waterline in order to prevent stains on the gleaming topsides, so check that these are clear and that the seacock, which should be fitted at the exit point, is working properly.

↓ *The galvanising on this swim platform is deteriorating and the fastenings are probably corroded.*

HANDRAILS

Rigid handrails along the tops of the coachroof and superstructure are often subject to the same type of stresses, especially as in rolling seas they may be all that is preventing the crew from going overboard. Handrails come in various forms: earlier boats may have wooden handrails, while in modern boats they are almost always constructed from stainless steel tubing. The securing fitting on stainless rails is welded into the supporting studs and here you need to grab the rail and exert pressure to determine whether there are any signs of movement. If there are, it may be a case of tightening up the securing nuts, provided that you can access them, although you may need to apply sealant into the joint first. You can use the same technique with wooden handrails but also look closely at the wooden plugs which are fitted over the securing bolt head in the handrail. The plugs are designed to hide the securing bolt heads but they may work loose and allow water into the hole where it can lie and start up corrosion in the bolts (unless they are stainless or bronze). At the very least, dig out the old plug and check the bolt head underneath before fitting a new plug and sealing the hole. Moreover, check the join where the wooden fitting meets the composite moulding to ensure there is no movement and a good seal, and the securing points below if you can get access to them. Finally, the handrail may be a simple wooden strip laid between and secured to raised points in the moulding: once again, check that these are secure.

DAVITS

Like stanchions, davits have a high leverage factor, with the tender suspended from the extremities of the davit, and they tend to be attached through base plates bolted to the hull or deck. They are designed with stress in mind and each davit should take on equal strain, but this is where problems can occur. For example, if davits are imbalanced on a tender outboard motor it can cause unequal loads, so be alert to stress cracks and strains around the attachment plates, both inside and out.

↓ Stress cracks are visible around the fastenings of this coachroof handrail.

↓ Judging by the gel coat cracks, this davit mounting is stressed.

WHY SURVEY YOUR OWN BOAT?

THE TOOLS OF THE TRADE

THE HULL

DECK AND SUPERSTRUCTURE

ENGINES AND THEIR SYSTEMS

STERN GEAR

PLUMBING

← The deck covering here could hide stress cracks below.

→ There are stress cracks around this auxiliary outboard mounting and impact damage above.

BOW FITTINGS

In your survey of the deck and super-structure you'll want to spend some time examining the fittings at the bow. The bow rollers that provide the lead for the anchor chain and sometimes the mooring ropes can be under considerable stress. Check that the bow rollers move freely and are not worn, but that they are free from too much play, which could indicate wear in the spindle bearings. You might want to knock this spindle pin out occasionally to examine it more closely. There is rarely any way to lubricate this spindle when installed so it needs to be fairly free running otherwise it could seize up if left unused for lengthy periods. This bow fitting will also be the anchorage for the forestay on sailboats, which can add to the stress, so you want to ensure it is in good condition.

ANCHOR CAPSTAN

The anchor capstan is usually a separate installation from the bow fitting and as this is the primary mooring point of the boat when at anchor, it needs careful examination. You may not be able to see the fixing bolts from the outside, so you'll have to dismantle the fitting or check it out from the inside. Any signs of movement should be examined in more detail and,

at the very least, the bolts hardened up.

Unless it is the hand operated type of capstan found on smaller boats, the capstan is usually operated by an electric motor located in the chain locker. This chain locker can be a breeding ground for damp conditions, so examine the electric motor and its connections for any signs of corrosion (see chapter 5). At the same time check the cable entries through the bulkhead where the electric cable comes into the chain locker. The wiring for this is quite substantial because of the heavy current it carries, so the cable entry should be fully watertight and sealed.

A survey is a good time to remove the entire anchor chain from the locker and check it for wear. This will give you a chance to clear any muck or debris that always accumulates in the chain locker and to check that the drain hole(s) at the bottom are clear. Doing this will also give you access to a part of the hull interior for a further visual check on the hull structure. Also, check the chain carefully, since this can be vital to your survival (see chapter 11 for further advice on checking the anchor and its chain).

↑ *The radar antenna is set too low on this boat so that the crew standing on the flybridge would obstruct the radar beam.*

← *There is a lot of detail to check out in the crowded bow area.*

↑ *Winch mounts are one of the areas where you may find stress cracks.*

WHY SURVEY YOUR OWN BOAT?

THE TOOLS OF THE TRADE

THE HULL

DECK AND SUPERSTRUCTURE

ENGINES AND THEIR SYSTEMS

STERN GEAR

PLUMBING

Deck and superstructure

SURVEY CHECKLIST

- ☐ Are the mouldings around high stress fittings free of crazing/cracking?
- ☐ Are all securing nuts and bolts on these fittings tight?
- ☐ Is an adequate backing plate fitted to these fittings?
- ☐ Are guard rails secure?
- ☐ Does a 'bounce' test show the coach roof to have integrity?
- ☐ Is the fender or rubbing strip at the deck edge secure?
- ☐ Are the scuppers free and is the deck free of any lying water?
- ☐ Are bends and corners of mouldings free of cracks?
- ☐ Do wooden decks have integrity?
- ☐ Are wooden decks free of water underneath?
- ☐ Are all the fairleads well secured and free of sharp edges that cause rope chafe?

5 ENGINES AND THEIR SYSTEMS

OPEN UP THE engine hatch on any boat and you get a pretty good idea of the state of the engine and its systems straight away. Oil leaks, dirt and corrosion should be immediately evident signs of either a poor level of maintenance or neglect, and can be a good indication of the boat's condition as a whole. On older boats there may be an acceptable level of deterioration in the engine area but you still need to differentiate between normal wear and tear and the sort of neglect that can lead to trouble.

A survey of the actual engine(s) and its performance (or lack thereof) is beyond the scope of the average surveyor and private owner, who has to take much of it for granted. Fortunately modern engines are incredibly reliable and the internals rarely fail. All you can really do is examine the exterior of both the engine and its systems and call in the experts if you're concerned. Of course, if it's your own boat you should already have a pretty good idea about the internals of the engine and the standards of maintenance carried out so far.

Engine compartments

IF YOU'RE CARRYING out a survey on a boat you're thinking of buying, opening up the engine compartment should be one of the first things you do once you have completed your outside examination. A neglected engine compartment is a depressing sight and it's reasonable to assume that if there's neglect here, there could well be comparable neglect around the rest of the boat, meaning you might want to walk away from this one. Here, the phrase 'out of sight, out of mind' comes to mind – as long as the engine starts and runs when asked, all is well. Actually, there's more to worry about than the engine cutting out at sea: a fault or failure in the engine compartment could lead to a fire or even the boat sinking. Only a detailed examination will give you the confidence to strike out to sea while carrying highly inflammable liquids and hot exhausts.

→ *Signs of serious salt water leaking on this inboard petrol engine.*

WHY SURVEY YOUR OWN BOAT?

THE TOOLS OF THE TRADE

THE HULL

DECK AND SUPERSTRUCTURE

ENGINES AND THEIR SYSTEMS

STERN GEAR

PLUMBING

ACCESS

To carry out this type of detailed examination during a survey you'll need access, which is easier said than done, since builders tend to assemble and install the engine compartment before the deck and superstructure mouldings. Many of the auxiliary systems on modern boats, such as air conditioning, water makers, generators, pumps and a host of small items, are often installed one at a time with the support systems hidden behind the later additions. It can be a complex web of pipework and wiring and it's likely you'll have to resort to mirrors and cameras to see what is going on. The sound proofing that is fitted in most engine compartments doesn't help either, and it can restrict access to parts of the hull as well as to some of the system's supporting pipes and wires. You won't be thanked if you feel the need to disturb this soundproof lining during your survey, but fortunately you can often get a pretty good impression of the standard of maintenance and the condition of fittings and fixtures by

↓ *Getting access to all parts of sailboat engines can be a challenge.*

examining those you can see. If these are in poor condition, the hidden bits are not likely to be any better.

Access to the engine compartment on sailboats can be particularly bad and while the designer or builder should have created access to the parts of the engine requiring routine maintenance, he may well have ignored it altogether for certain parts of the cooling system or the exhaust. Moreover, in order to maximise space for the accommodation, the engine box has usually suffered and is tightly fitted around the engine so that access to many parts can only be achieved with some dismantling of the surrounding structure. Things get slightly better when the engine compartment extends to the full width of the hull but even then the fuel tanks may have been installed at the side, meaning access to them is even more restricted. Such is the demand for space on modern boats, I've even seen engines in which it is impossible to get to the fresh water cooling system cap to top up the coolant without removing sealed down sections of the engine compartment. With this in mind, you'll need to be something of a contortionist to get into the more remote parts of the engine compartment, and while a mirror on a stick or camera may help you to see what is going on, you do lose the ability to touch and feel pipework and fittings. It goes without saying that in a situation such as this, any repairs become next to impossible without major removals.

MAIN SYSTEMS AND MOUNTS

This might all seem pretty depressing, but there is one thing in your favour when it comes to modern engines and that is they

← *That stain in the bilge could be an indication of a water leak.*

↑ *A good quality installation with excellent engine access.*

are incredibly reliable and any problems are much more likely to come from the support systems rather than the engine itself. You can examine these engine support systems to a considerable degree during a survey and certainly if you are examining your own boat you'll want to check them in as much detail as possible.

You'll need to assess the four main systems: the oil and cooling water levels, the flexible drive belts and the outside of the engine. If you find low oil or water levels, this could be a warning sign of poor maintenance, which should make you reconsider progressing further with this boat. When you check the oil level take a close look at what is on the end of the dip stick; a sort of light coloured emulsion could be a sign of water in the engine. If there is oil on the outside of the engine there's probably also oil in the bilges, which would indicate a possible oil leak. This might be acceptable on older engines, since seals were not up to the standards found on modern engines (older engines were usually painted a dark colour so oil leaks would be less obvious). However, any evidence of an oil leak on a modern engine could mean it's time to call for an expert opinion or walk away, although do consider that the stain might have come from a

WHY SURVEY YOUR OWN BOAT?

THE TOOLS OF THE TRADE

THE HULL

DECK AND SUPERSTRUCTURE

ENGINES AND THEIR SYSTEMS

STERN GEAR

PLUMBING

→ It may look old and tired but the basic engine can be sound.

↓ Oil stains where this engine has been removed are a strong indication of trouble.

there are no signs of movement between the engine mounting plates and the engine beds; on a composite boat, this is indicated by minor signs of wear, while on a metal boat the engine bed will have small shiny areas. On steel engine beds there may be the giveaway sign of a cocoa-like powder, which indicates slight movement between steel sections that may be corroded to a

spillage during topping up of the engine oil.

The engine drive belts, which power the water pumps and alternator, should have a small degree of play in them, perhaps 1–2cm of up and down movement on a horizontal section of the belt. Anything more than this and the belt will need to be adjusted, which is usually achieved by adjusting the alternator mounting or a special adjusting pulley in the system.

At this point you'll also want to look at the engine mounts. Some engines, mainly in older boats and in work and fishing boats, are solidly mounted, i.e. bolted directly onto the engine beds with no flexibility. These should be checked to ensure that

↓ There can be a lot to check in a compact engine installation like this.

degree. Any sign of movement is easily cured by tightening the securing nuts and bolts.

You should not see any signs of wear in the flexible mounts found on many modern installations, except perhaps in the rubber mouldings which give the mount its flexibility. These should be intact and free of deterioration such as splits or wear. If you come across these signs, then replacement is the only solution. A boat with a flexibly mounted engine should have much less vibration, but you do end up with a more complex system overall since all of the connections to the engine also require flexible sections in their pipework and wiring.

So much for the engine itself, now it's time to look at the systems that supply and support the engine in more detail, since this is where you're much more likely to find signs of potential problems.

Fuel systems

YOU NEED TO go back to the beginning when checking the fuel system. The main components here are the fuel tank itself, the fuel lines and valves, and the filters.

THE FUEL TANK

Fuel tanks come in many shapes and sizes and may be constructed of composite, steel, stainless steel and aluminium. As we have said, composite tanks tend to be integrated into the hull moulding with perhaps only the top of the tank visible. Integral tanks look very neat and tidy but they suffer from the fact that they cannot be drained and there is unlikely to be a sump built

in to the bottom of the tank where any dirt and water in the fuel can collect and possibly be drained off. Metal tanks should have this facility but a lot depends on how they're installed and what level of access is available around the tank. If you can get to a drain tap, run off some of the fuel/water mix from the bottom of the tank to check for contamination; small amounts of water and debris are permissible but when considerable amounts have to be run off before clean fuel comes through, this suggests a lack of basic maintenance.

A tank full of fuel is a considerable weight and the mounts do come under some stress, so you'll need to examine the securing systems for the tanks. As with the engine mounts, you're looking for any signs of movement and/or stress. Where metal straps secure the tanks to their mounting points, look for those same shiny metal areas.

It's likely that the connections to the tank will be made through a top plate, which can also act as a manhole cover for access to the tank's interior. The plate will be secured with many nuts and bolts, making its removal a time consuming act, but if you have the time to spare, doing so will allow you to shine a torch into the interior to see what lies in the bottom of the tank. If you do decide to remove the manhole plate, take extra care if the tank contains petrol because there can be an explosive atmosphere in the empty part of the tank and you don't want to cause an explosion with a spark from your tools. Diesel fuel is relatively safe but do not poke your head inside (if the hole is large enough) because it doesn't contain breathable air. In any case, you'll perhaps

WHY SURVEY YOUR OWN BOAT?

THE TOOLS OF THE TRADE

THE HULL

DECK AND SUPERSTRUCTURE

ENGINES AND THEIR SYSTEMS

STERN GEAR

PLUMBING

↑ All the pipes and connections on the top of the fuel tank need checking.

↑ Fuel tank fittings come in many shapes and sizes.

be more concerned with the connections themselves, such as the filler and suction pipe and the fuel level connection, so check these are tight and sound with no obvious leakage.

As far as you can, check the outside of the tank for signs of leakage, which is most likely to come from minute cracks in the welding (focus on the seams). With diesel, fuel leaks will be evident through staining, but leaked petrol fuel evaporates so you may not see anything. Your sense of smell can come into play here but don't rely on it, as there's usually always a slight smell of petrol or diesel around the engine and tank area. However, a strong smell should definitely be tracked to its source.

LINES AND PIPES

The filler pipe connects the tank to the outside filler, which will usually be on one of the side decks or possibly in the cockpit on a sailboat. It may not be possible to get a view of the connection between the deck fitting and the filler, but it's not critical since the filler spout goes into the hose.

It is, however, critical that you get a look at the lower end of the tank with the hose and spigot, as any leak here will deposit fuel inside the boat. Look for staining, especially at the top joint and running down the filler pipe. This filler pipe is of generous dimensions in order to take the flow from the fuel pump nozzle, and it goes without saying that it should be made from a fuel resistant material. If there are two tanks there will often be an equalising pipe

↓ Check all the fuel pipes and valves for any signs of leakage.

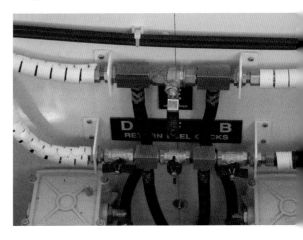

WHY SURVEY YOUR OWN BOAT?

THE TOOLS OF THE TRADE

THE HULL

DECK AND SUPERSTRUCTURE

ENGINES AND THEIR SYSTEMS

STERN GEAR

PLUMBING

connecting the two so that both tanks can be filled from one deck connection. A valve will control the connection between the two tanks.

A run of piping with valves controls the volume of fuel from the tank to the engine, so check all pipework, valves and joints for leaks using sight, smell and touch; leaking diesel fuel in particular has a distinctive slippery feel. Check any sight tube fuel gauges (usually a clear pipe with valves, mounted vertically on the tank and connected to the tank top and bottom). These gauges are the most reliable indication of the tank contents.

The length of flexible pipe built into the delivery fuel pipe to the engine, which allows for the movement of flexible mounts,

↓ The clear plastic fuel level sight gauge should be fitted with shut off valves in case of leaks or damage.

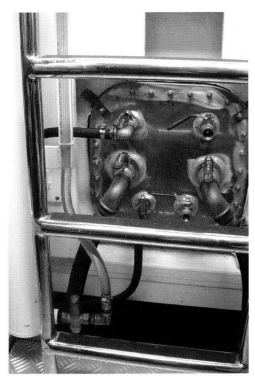

requires particular scrutiny. There shouldn't be a problem with modern equipment but on older boats the well-supported stainless steel or copper piping may have been replaced with unsupported piping, perhaps with lengths of plastic tubing and corroded jubilee clips. On sailboats and smaller single-engine boats there can be a long run from the fuel tank to the engine and here the pipe may be unsecured and left to its own devices, possibly coming to rest in the bilges. This can be a recipe for disaster and if the pipe fractures or leaks and there is a gravity feed to the engine, it may not be noticed until the tank has run dry. These are all curable problems and should not necessarily condemn a boat but they could be indications of a casual attitude to safety, which could extend to other areas of the boat.

Leaks in a petrol system require immediate attention, which usually means tightening the joints. If that doesn't solve the problem turn off the fuel at the tank and seek assistance: there may well be fuel vapour in the bilges resulting from the leak, which can be an explosive mixture.

FILTERS

Filters are an essential part of the fuel system and there are usually two in each fuel line, one external and one as part of the engine. Older types of external filters often had a glass bowl so that you could see any contamination or water in the fuel as it separated out. On closed filters you can open them up to check that there is no excess contamination, which would indicate that there could be a lot of dirt in the bottom of the fuel tank. Many older fuel filters were primarily designed for use on

71

land in trucks and made from aluminium, which tends to corrode in the marine environment. While this type of corrosion may not be serious, it does need to be checked.

One very modern problem is the growth of 'diesel bug', a microbiological growth that infests diesel and can cause considerable trouble if it is allowed to develop. Modern diesel fuel has a reduced amount of sulphur, a chemical addition which was used to deter the bug, and we are also seeing increased amounts of bio-diesel entering modern fuel supplies, so while these might be 'greener', there is a penalty to pay as diesel bug can clog up fuel pipes and filters and, if it gets as far as the engine itself, the injectors. It manifests itself as a sort of dark jelly-like growth, although it can be difficult to find as it tends to accumulate in the areas that are not visible.

So where should you be looking? The bug tends to start at the interface between

↑ *This aluminium casting on the top of this fuel filter is badly corroded.*

the diesel fuel and any water in the fuel. All diesel contains a certain amount of water and this usually settles out in the tank where it can be drained off, which should be a routine part of the boat's maintenance. The problems start when there are no drain cocks on the tank, since the tank is in the bottom of the boat so there is no access to a drain even if one is fitted. Draining the water should prevent

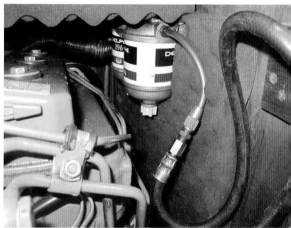

← *A good fuel filter installation with double hose clips.*

↑ *Getting access to these fuel filters could be challenging.*

the bug developing, but you're not here to perform maintenance, you're here to find defects, so the best place to look for a diesel bug infestation is in the fuel filter. The jelly-like substance may be fluid enough to flow through the early stages of the fuel pipe, but then it hits the filter and gets another chance to develop, since the chances are that there will be a fuel/water interface in this filter. If you spot diesel bug here, you're in with a chance of solving the problem before it gets any worse by either draining the fuel tank and cleaning it or using one of the proprietary fuel additives that are designed to eradicate the bug. If the bug has had a chance to get into the engine, you'll want to think carefully about buying the boat as it's a tricky problem to eradicate. If you're surveying your own boat you'll know if the bug has reached the engine because it will either be running erratically or stop altogether. All modern engines feature a second stage prevention system, the fine particle filters fitted to the engine itself. If you find evidence of the bug here and the engine is still running, you have probably caught the problem in time and you should dismantle and clean the fuel system back to the tank from here. If the problem has reached the engine, be prepared for considerable dismantling, not to mention expense.

While the fuel system is a vital part of the boat's systems the only part that could present a major concern is the fuel tank; otherwise, it can be a relatively simple job to bring a poor fuel system up to date. If the boat is fuelled by petrol, it is a requirement of both insurance companies and official rules and regulations that you have a high quality fuel system installed.

↑ *The sludge in this filter is the result of diesel bug.*

Cooling systems

THE ENGINE COOLING system is another vital part of the boat; not only could a failure cause the engine to stop or become damaged, but since the whole of the sea water part of the cooling system is directly connected to the sea, if a hose fails or there is some other leak it could cause a flood and the boat could sink! This is why only the highest standard is permissible.

↑ *A good installation of twin water filters.*

WHY SURVEY YOUR OWN BOAT?

THE TOOLS OF THE TRADE

THE HULL

DECK AND SUPERSTRUCTURE

ENGINES AND THEIR SYSTEMS

STERN GEAR

PLUMBING

There is yet one more potential cooling system emergency: On most installations the sea water exiting from the engine is injected into the exhaust pipe, thereby cooling the exhaust gases on their way out so that they don't melt the flexible rubber sections of the exhaust. If that water injection into the exhaust fails, hot exhaust gases are directly released onto the rubber piping and the best you can hope for is that the rubber will just melt. In a worst-case (and most likely) scenario the rubber will catch fire, meaning you could be faced with the double whammy of having the boat sinking from water ingress and catching fire through exhaust pipe failure. At least the incoming water might put out the fire! All this should be enough to convince you to check out the sea water side of the cooling system very, very carefully.

You may still find direct cooling systems on older boats, in which the sea water circulates directly around the engine to cool it, but modern engines have an indirect cooling system, in which the sea water passes through a heat exchanger where it cools the closed fresh water system that circulates around the engine. This gives a more consistent cooling of the engine and also removes the corrosive sea water from sensitive parts of the engine interior. On both systems there are likely to be anodes fitted inside the engine and on associated pipework to reduce the possibility of electrolytic action between different metals.

COOLING SYSTEM SURVEY ROUTINE

Chapter 7 covers seacocks in detail, so let's start at the hose connected to the seacocks. Here you would expect to find double hose clips securing the hose in position, and these should be free of corrosion. Some types of stainless steel are not resistant to sea water so the clips should ideally be proper marine grade types. Check that they are actually located fully over the seacock spigot because you can sometimes find the second clip teetering on the edge or unevenly tightened.

Next, check the hose itself to ensure there are no signs of swelling, which you would see around the outer securing clip. Any sign of swelling in the hose is a sign

↓ The drive belts and the water pump are critical parts of the engine.

↓ Double worm drive clips should be fitted to every connection in the cooling system.

that it is deteriorating and needs replacing. If replacement is needed, make sure you use the highest quality rubber hose designed for the purpose and that you avoid plastic, which can harden and crack.

Follow the same routine around each of the sea water hoses where they connect with and leave the engine. You will find some that are actually an integral part of the engine, so follow the engine manufacturer's recommendations regarding their replacement, unless you find that they look suspect. A sensible precaution would be to replace the connections to the seacock and filter every two years, even if there are no visible signs of deterioration. The filter unit can be a weak point in the cooling system and is often constructed from clear plastic so that you can see any muck or debris that has collected. However, rigid plastic is often brittle and easily damaged when knocked. Therefore, check the filter for any signs of cracking and the contents for any signs of debris.

Seacocks for the engine cooling water system are usually located in the bottom of the boat, which helps to ensure continuity

↓ Checking the water filter for any debris.

of the cooling water supply if the boat is moving in waves but it also means they are the first thing to get covered in water if the system springs a leak. It can be a challenge trying to find them underwater, so you may want to consider fitting an extension to the valve spindle, or another means of turning them off that will be well above any incoming water or even above decks. When underway you won't immediately see any leak in the cooling system in the enclosed engine compartment, so you may consider fitting an early warning flow sensor. This should be fitted in the exhaust end of the system otherwise you could have a leak where the sensor would not sound the warning.

Exhaust systems

THE ENGINE EXHAUST system is just as critical as the rest of the engine systems and defects here could lead to the engine compartment flooding and exhaust fumes entering the boat. Even a small leak in the pipework may release fumes that could build up to poisonous levels of carbon monoxide and if a crewmember is sleeping in the aft cabin on a sailboat, he/she could be vulnerable.

In addition to removing exhaust gases the exhaust system usually channels the sea water cooling away. Combine the corrosive characteristics of exhaust gases with those of sea water and the exhaust system comes in for considerable abuse, particularly as parts of it are often hidden when it comes to a routine inspection. To check the exhaust you need to track the whole length of the piping, which on a sailboat could be quite a length running along in the bilges.

WHY SURVEY YOUR OWN BOAT?

THE TOOLS OF THE TRADE

THE HULL

DECK AND SUPERSTRUCTURE

ENGINES AND THEIR SYSTEMS

STERN GEAR

PLUMBING

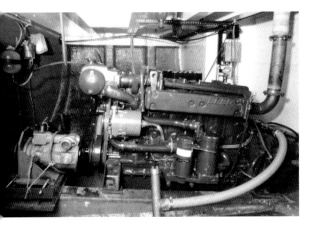

← Single clips and the plastic hose on the water intake of this engine would make this installation suspect.

→ A salt encrusted exhaust pipe suggests leaks from the cooling water in the exhaust.

Today, it is usual to find the exhaust system comprises a reinforced flexible pipe which connects the exhaust elbow on the engine to the outlet pipe in the hull. This outlet might be underwater, since this can help to reduce the noise levels of the exhaust, or it could be just above the waterline. Either way there will be the risk of water finding its way in if there is any leak and this is one outlet in the hull where you are unlikely to find a seacock. The layout of the exhaust pipe should be such that water cannot find its way back up the pipe and into the engine and this means it will often have an anti-siphon elbow built in. A silencer might also be included in the system.

To survey the exhaust, look for external signs of deterioration in the fixed and flexible sections of the pipework. The flexible rubber pipe has to be of the highest standard since it has to cope with both heat and sea water: any signs of swelling or softness in the rubber should ring alarm bells. This can be particularly apparent at connections and joints and the worm drive clips used for these connections should be free of corrosion or deterioration. Like most of the engine cooling systems there should

be double clips at these connections. Any signs of white crystals showing at the clips, connections and joints would indicate a sea water leak.

Hydraulics

TODAY HYDRAULIC SYSTEMS, either hand or engine powered, are a feature of many boats. On sailboats you may find hand hydraulics used for the backstay tightening and for the vang, while engine powered hydraulics may power the thruster(s) and a passerelle. Many steering systems are also based on hydraulic systems, which translate the wheel movements into the actions of the hydraulic ram that operates the tiller arm. On engine powered hydraulic systems the hydraulic pump is usually attached to the engine side of the gearbox and will include an oil tank, perhaps a cooler, the control valves and the pipework.

Hydraulic systems are usually fully self-contained and reliable, so your survey should focus on possible oil leaks and corrosion. Oil leaks may not be easily visible but you can quickly feel any oil by rubbing your hand along the pipework and around the joints. Check that the oil tank level is reasonably full (which, as we now know, is a sign of good maintenance). Examine the ferules around the joints; standard hydraulic hoses are designed primarily for land use and are usually constructed from plated steel, which doesn't stand up well to the marine environment, so it's likely you'll find light corrosion here. It's not necessarily a serious problem unless the corrosion has developed into serious rust, in which case it might be time to replace the hoses. Any swelling or softness in the flexible sections of hose should be viewed with suspicion and is likely to require replacement. Hoses, both flexible and rigid, in the hydraulic system should be supported to prevent chafe and wear, so check clips and restraints, particularly in hidden areas if you can get to them. While hydraulic system failures are not likely to be life-threatening, they are generally a job for the experts, so could turn out to be expensive should you decide to go ahead with the purchase of the boat.

Generators

GENERATORS ARE NOW a common installation on many modern motorboats, since they supply power for cooking and air conditioning units. Because the generator is usually housed in a soundproof box it can be a case of out of sight, out of mind. Generator operation is not usually critical to the safety of a boat, although like the main engine(s), the diesel engine section of the generator has the potential to flood the boat if there is a failure in its sea water cooling system. In fact, the situation could be much worse; a main engine failure is likely to be detected much sooner, but a generator could be running overnight when everyone on board is fast asleep and you'll only discover there's been a failure when your feet get wet!

We'll look at the electrical aspects of generators in more detail in chapter 9, but suffice to say detailed checks are vital when you are dealing with the high voltages associated with this piece of equipment. Therefore, your survey should include just as close an examination of the generator and its systems as that of the main engine, so be sure to trace the associated pipework and fuel systems and remove the covers to inspect the engine.

→ *Marine growth on this bow thruster would make it less efficient.*

Engine

SURVEY CHECKLIST

- ☐ Is the exterior clean and free of signs of oil leaks?
- ☐ Is it free of signs of corrosion?
- ☐ Are the engine mounts free of signs of movement?
- ☐ Is the fuel system free of leaks?
- ☐ Are the cooling water pipes in good condition?
- ☐ Are the hose clips in good condition?
- ☐ Does the exhaust look sound and is it free of leaks?
- ☐ Are electrical connections in good condition?

WHY SURVEY YOUR OWN BOAT?

THE TOOLS OF THE TRADE

THE HULL

DECK AND SUPERSTRUCTURE

ENGINES AND THEIR SYSTEMS

STERN GEAR

PLUMBING

6 STERN GEAR

STERN GEAR IS so often out of sight, out of mind, to the point that it is probably one of the most neglected areas in boat maintenance. Boats can go a whole season or more without anyone sighting and checking the stern gear and yet this can be one of the most critical parts of a boat, since any neglect can quickly lead to disaster. Obviously the boat has to be out of the water to survey the stern gear and all boat owners should take every opportunity (for example, when the boat has been lifted out for a quick paint or it has just dried out over a tide) to check it.

There are two aspects to any failure in the stern gear. First, you may lose either the propulsion or the steering or possibly both, which can immobilise the boat in a way that may be difficult or impossible to fix at sea. Second, a failure could lead to water getting into the boat, which will add to the drama of the situation! So the moral is, don't take any chances with the stern gear when you inspect it and take special care over it when you do.

Propeller and shaft

LET'S LOOK AT the propeller and its shaft first, since virtually every boat, both power and sail, will have this in one form or another. One of the simplest propulsion installations is an outboard motor and the benefit here is that there are no through-hull openings to be sealed. On a larger outboard powered boat you should check the areas around the engine mounting because this can be under considerable stress at times and you may find some cracking of the gel coat to indicate this (see chapter 12 for further advice on surveying outboards).

SUPPORT AND BEARINGS

For boats with a conventional shaft and propeller system you need to examine several areas. First, try lifting the propeller and its shaft and moving it to and fro at the propeller end. Any movement indicates

← The stern gear looks sound at first glance but a detailed check is required.

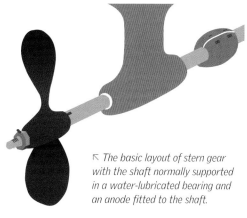

↖ The basic layout of stern gear with the shaft normally supported in a water-lubricated bearing and an anode fitted to the shaft.

WHY SURVEY YOUR OWN BOAT?

THE TOOLS OF THE TRADE

THE HULL

DECK AND SUPERSTRUCTURE

ENGINES AND THEIR SYSTEMS

STERN GEAR

PLUMBING

there is wear in the shaft bearings or the shaft itself, and if you find it here move on to the P-bracket, which supports the shaft close to the propeller, and perform the same test. P-bracket bearings are usually hard rubber with grooves in the rubber which allow water to flow through, lubricating the bearing. A small amount of movement is normal here because obviously the rubber cannot be a tight fit around the shaft, but any excessive movement, say more than a couple of millimetres, could indicate bearing wear and requires further inspection.

The shaft and bearing can take a lot of abuse, particularly in water where there is a lot of suspended sediment, leading to abrasive material flowing through the bearing. The hard rubber bearing is designed to clear this debris, and it works very well, but if it is showing signs of wear it won't get any better. You'll need to establish whether the wear is in the bearing or on the shaft itself, which could mean removing the propeller, releasing the grub screws that hold the bearing housing in place and sliding it out, which should

also give you a view of the area of the shaft that lies in the bearing.

The bearings are generally very reliable and do not wear a great deal, so if you find excessive movement in the propeller shaft the chances are it will be a shaft rather than a bearing problem. If you do need to replace a bearing it is a relatively simple job. However, if the shaft is the issue you'll need a specialist to build it up again to its original diameter. Before you go too far down this line check the inlets that allow water to flow into the bearing; on an exposed P-bracket the natural flow of water into the bearing creates the lubrication, but if a rope cutter is fitted it can impede or reduce the flow, which can cause excessive wear.

On sailboats you often find that the propeller shaft emerges directly from the deadwood or the hull moulding with the propeller attached directly to the stub of the exposed shaft without a P-bracket or other support. The shaft support bearing may be a water-lubricated bearing fitted with small scoops on either side that direct the water into the bearing. These can get

↓ *That scoop channels water into the shaft bearing to lubricate it, so ensure the scoop is clear of debris and barnacles.*

↓ *Check the propeller shaft for any movement that would indicate bearing wear.*

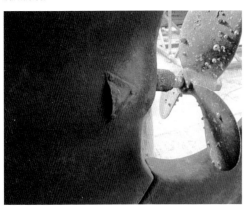

↑ This anode is going to need to be renewed soon.

↑ It is important to take the opportunity to check all the stern gear when the boat is out of the water.

WHY SURVEY YOUR OWN BOAT?

THE TOOLS OF THE TRADE

THE HULL

DECK AND SUPERSTRUCTURE

ENGINES AND THEIR SYSTEMS

STERN GEAR

PLUMBING

clogged with barnacles or other growth, so if they're present, check they're clear and functioning. (While marine growth is usually cleaned off when the boat is taken out of the water, it may be difficult to clear in the hard-to-reach areas, so growth on any propulsion system/the rudder could signal low standards of maintenance in general.)

Alternatively, the support bearing can be inside the hull where it may be water lubricated through a pipe attached to the bearing. Finally, and only usually on older boats, it could be a grease lubricated bearing with a screw down cap (you can often detect a grease type bearing from the outside because of oil stains around the point where the shaft exits the hull). If there is movement found in the propeller shaft with one of these installations, you need to explore inside the boat. It may be a case of withdrawing the shaft to check its condition and that of the bearing, which is obviously tricky. It could even mean taking out the engine and gearbox first so that the shaft can be withdrawn into the boat or, alternatively, it may be possible to disconnect the coupling on the shaft and

remove the shaft from the stern, although this may entail removing the rudder first.

STERN GLANDS

Inside shaft bearings are usually combined with a stern gland, which is what keeps the water from entering the boat around the rotating shaft. The stern gland plays a vital role and if the boat is afloat, it should be checked for any dripping water coming into the hull around the shaft. Checking this function with the boat ashore can be difficult, but if someone turns the shaft while you watch it closely you may be able to detect distortion in the bearing, which could lead to leaking and also produce excessive vibration when under way. On

↓ A well-fitted stern gland waiting for the lubricating water connection.

↑ *A traditional grease lubricated stern gland.*

and the shaft to ensure smooth running, and an alternative flexing joint may be included in the drive train to allow for any slight misalignment. Flexing joints come in many shapes and sizes, such as a mechanical joint of the universal joint type or the more popular type that incorporates rubber sections to help reduce vibration and allow for the movement of a flexibly mounted engine. With either type, check for any wear in the joint by trying to rotate the shaft against the fixed engine. On the rubber type check the rubber for any signs of ageing such as cracks in the surface.

An alternative type of stern gland has the shaft passing through a tube in the hull where it is supported by an outboard bearing. To seal the joint around the shaft a short length of rubber hose is attached to the inside section of the hull tube with its other end coupled to the sealing gland. Such an installation can allow for some

older boats it may just be the grease forced into the bearing that is preventing water from entering, so check the shaft for any up and down or sideways movement.

Some stern glands are mounted rigid with the hull and also act as a bearing to support the shaft. This type of installation requires careful alignment of the engine

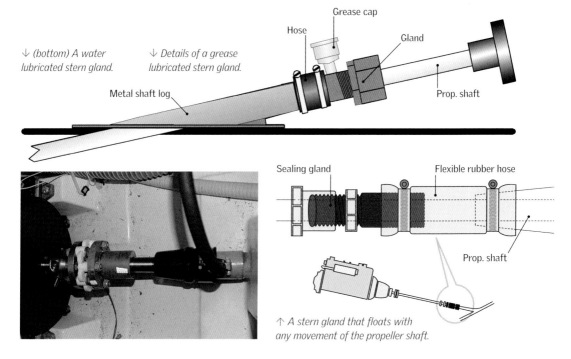

↓ *(bottom) A water lubricated stern gland.*

↓ *Details of a grease lubricated stern gland.*

Grease cap

Hose

Gland

Metal shaft log

Prop. shaft

Sealing gland

Flexible rubber hose

Prop. shaft

↑ *A stern gland that floats with any movement of the propeller shaft.*

↑ *The shaft here looks off centre from its exit hole perhaps indicating bearing wear.*

↑ *That gap in the P-bracket looks serious, but there are separate shaft bearing support and bracket units bolted together.*

movement in the shaft without causing leaks but it relies heavily on the rubber hose and its securing clips to keep the water out. This is a critical bit of hose and it should be checked for any swelling or softness. Ensure there are double clips and that they are free of corrosion, which is more likely on the difficult-to-see parts of the clips underneath the tube. There should be a renewal programme for this hose section just like that for the engine cooling water hoses, but fitting a new section means disconnecting the flange or flexible joint that connects the shaft to the gearbox and drawing the shaft out. If there is a need to dismantle this stern seal system do take the opportunity to inspect the condition of the shaft in the bearing for wear.

It's quite easy to check for wear in the propeller shafts of most sailboats and smaller motorboats, but on a planing powerboat the size and weight of the shafts and propellers make it difficult to detect any movement when you try to move them. The only solution here, short of dismantling, is a detailed visual inspection: look for bearings that are slightly oval in

shape or signs of weeping oil or water at the points at which the shaft log leaves the hull. It's difficult to say how much wear is acceptable but if you can see a bearing that is oval rather than round, it requires further attention.

Integrated drive systems

WHILE SHAFTS AND propellers are the main type of drive system found on boats, there is a growing trend towards integrated drive systems such as stern drives, sail drives and pod drives. In each of these systems the whole drive train is fully enclosed and you can't see what is happening inside without stripping it down. You could check for undue wear or play in the system by putting the drive in gear and trying to turn the propeller. The very nature of the system means there will always be a certain amount of play, but alarm bells should ring if you have trouble turning the propeller by anything less than a significant amount.

WHY SURVEY YOUR OWN BOAT?

THE TOOLS OF THE TRADE

THE HULL

DECK AND SUPERSTRUCTURE

ENGINES AND THEIR SYSTEMS

STERN GEAR

PLUMBING

↑ Marine growth on this sail drive is partially blocking the water intake and may upset the operation of the feather propeller.

↓ You need to check the sealing fittings where this sail drive exits the hull.

hole, and this is where you should look for trouble. To reduce vibration and make for simpler installation the hole is usually sealed with a rubber gasket, or perhaps even two for security. Inspect these rubber gaskets for any signs of wear or perhaps cracking in the rubber, which could signal that they are nearing the end of their useful life. The manufacturers will probably propose renewal after a fixed period, perhaps ten years as a safety measure.

On sail drives the rubber gaskets are often held in place by large worn drive clips and this is where you should focus your checks for the usual corrosion/damage. The seal where the drive exits the hull is critical to the safety of the boat so even though access can be difficult, do not skimp on this check.

ANODES

Since they often comprise an aluminium casting combined with bronze propellers or other forms of dissimilar metals, each of these integrated drive systems has anodes built into it to protect it from electrolytic corrosion. Anodes are designed so that they, rather than critical parts of the boat, are attacked and eroded, so it is pretty easy to detect corrosion. The anodes may be in the form of a ring around the hub of the propeller unit or in the propeller cone; check them for excessive erosion, which indicates that not only are they doing their job properly but – especially if they are more than half eroded – this could be the time for renewal (note that anodes should not be painted, since it is the exposed bare metal that allows them to do their job).

Boats with conventional propulsion systems will also be fitted with anodes of

Stern drives are bolted to the transom and their outboard legs are designed to lift up for stowage or in the event of grounding. Flexible connections are built into the drive shaft and the exhaust, while you'll also need to examine the integrity of the exhaust piping. Check the hydraulic cylinders that do the lifting for any signs of leakage, which you'll be able to feel when wiping your hand along the pipes or rams.

Beyond stern drives, the other drive systems exit through the hull via a sealed

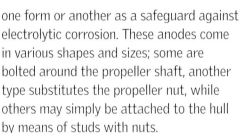

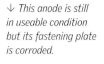

← This propeller is showing signs of wear or damage.

↓ This anode is still in useable condition but its fastening plate is corroded.

WHY SURVEY YOUR OWN BOAT?

THE TOOLS OF THE TRADE

THE HULL

DECK AND SUPERSTRUCTURE

ENGINES AND THEIR SYSTEMS

STERN GEAR

PLUMBING

one form or another as a safeguard against electrolytic corrosion. These anodes come in various shapes and sizes; some are bolted around the propeller shaft, another type substitutes the propeller nut, while others may simply be attached to the hull by means of studs with nuts.

In steel and aluminium hulls where there are vast expanses of metal, anodes are even more vital, so do the same checks for erosion, and anything less than half its original size calls for replacement. It would be nice to think that it's simply a question of unbolting the old one and bolting on a new one but the securing nuts will often be a struggle to remove – it often means cutting the bolts off and replacing them with new ones.

Inside the boat the various metal fittings and anodes should be linked together with an earthing wire or be in direct contact for the whole system to do its job; check these wire connections because they could be lying in the bilge and the inevitable corrosion in the copper wire and metal fitting can lead to the connection parting company.

ELECTROLYSIS

Electrolysis has been something of a nightmare in the past but we now have a much better understanding of why it occurs and how to prevent it. However, this does remain a specialist area and if you have any doubts regarding the deterioration of anodes, call the expert or simply walk away.

Electrolytic action is usually revealed through pitting in metal surfaces, just like you see in the anodes. The action dezincifies the bronze (attacks the zinc in the bronze as the soft option), which you may see in often pinkish-tinged pitting over the surface of the propeller. Since propellers are usually bronze or stern drives and sail drives on outboards aluminium

↑ *Electrolytic action and poor quality stainless steel have both caused this propeller shaft to become very badly pitted.*

↑ *The bottom end of this aluminium stern drive has been badly eroded by electrolytic action.*

alloy, chances are you'll see this type of pitting upon examination. And, in fact, this can reveal a lot about the boat's general condition: spot pitting here and you're likely to find it over most of the surface. You may well be looking at a replacement propeller, but consult an expert for help in finding the root cause of the pitting

before you go down that route. Examine the anodes and the earthing wires over the interior – is there any wiring that bypasses the main battery switch, which could have been earthed and created stray currents? Any time a boat is connected to a mains supply in the marina the earthing must be meticulous to avoid current leaks.

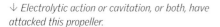

↓ *Electrolytic action or cavitation, or both, have attacked this propeller.*

↓ *This propeller looks okay but the marine growth will reduce the efficiency.*

↑ *This stern drive looks to be in poor condition but it is nothing that a good clean will not cure.*

OTHER PROPELLER DAMAGE

Damage to the tips or outer edge of the propeller could have been caused by grounding or striking debris in the water. Either way, any bent or damaged blades may create vibration, adding stress to the entire propulsion system and making life on board uncomfortable! It may be possible to straighten up small areas of tip bending and if bits have actually broken away, propeller specialists can build up the metal again.

Polishing on the propeller, revealed by shiny surfaces, could indicate that the owner has operated the boat in very shallow water or has perhaps grounded it on a sandy bottom, where the contact has polished the blades rather than damaged them. This is more likely to be seen on aluminium alloy propellers on outboards or stern drives rather than on bronze propellers where any shine will quickly disappear with further use. Propeller cavitation may be found on the propellers of faster boats, usually indicated by areas of polished or pitted blades. Severe pitting calls for a replacement propeller but, again,

it's worth calling in the expert before you take action.

Propellers are expensive bits of kit and you do not want to lose one at sea. Check that the propeller nut(s) are tight up against the propeller. There should be some way of locking the main nut tight to prevent it coming off at sea – it may be a second locking nut or simply a cotter pin that fits through a hole in the shaft and then into slots in the outer edge of the nut. While you are doing this also check that the P-bracket is secure to the hull; it is usually bolted through the hull. Slight movement will show through thin breaks in the antifouling paint around the edge of the plate that is fixed to the hull or around the securing bolt heads. If you see that thin break it could also be caused by vibration rather than a loose fitting, which could indicate that the shaft bearings are worn or the propeller has been damaged. It may be possible to

↓ *This polished aluminium propeller is the result of grounding or operating in sandy conditions.*

WHY SURVEY YOUR OWN BOAT?

THE TOOLS OF THE TRADE

THE HULL

DECK AND SUPERSTRUCTURE

ENGINES AND THEIR SYSTEMS

STERN GEAR

PLUMBING

↑ *This stern drive is suffering from electrolytic action and has dissimilar metals between the hub and the blades, a recipe for disaster.*

tighten up the bolts from the inside, but it would be best to withdraw the bolts and re-seal the flange.

FEATHERING PROPELLERS

Sailboats often have a feathering propeller installed. This is designed to reduce the drag when under sail and the propeller is not being used. There's a variety of

feathering propellers on the market, some two-bladed and some with three blades. On most designs they can be opened and closed by hand, so during a survey you can check the propeller's operation and that there is no undue play in the blade attachment, which would indicate wear in the support bearings. Certain designs have an oil-filled hull to support the blades so be alert to oil leaks around the hub. Feathering propellers are common on sail drives and, with an aluminium alloy drive leg and a bronze or stainless steel propeller, there can be a risk of electrolytic action between the two; check the drive anodes for excessive corrosion.

WATER JET PROPULSION

Some fast powerboats may have more exotic forms of propulsion such as water jets or surface drives. These systems often have exposed hydraulics that you'll need to check for leaks and corrosion, and in the case of surface drives there may be

↓ *This sail drive looks to be in sound condition.*

→ *A controllable pitch propeller needs very close checking because of the complex mechanism.*

an external gear box to examine. Water jets are vulnerable to marine growth inside the jet tunnel, which of course reduces the effectiveness of the propulsion; on smaller jets with restricted access it can be very hard to clear.

SURVEY CHECKLIST

Engine

- ☐ Are the propeller nut and locking device in good order?
- ☐ Are the shaft bearings secure?
- ☐ Are the bearing water scoops clear?
- ☐ Does the shaft have good fore and aft movement?
- ☐ Is the P-bracket secure?
- ☐ Are anodes attached to the shaft in good condition?
- ☐ Is the pitting on the blades free of electrolytic action?
- ☐ Is the blade tip free of damage?
- ☐ Is the propeller free of marine growth?

Rudder

WHILE THE DRIVE system propels the boat the rudder is your steering control, and one won't work without the other. However, in many cases the steering system does not get the same attention and maintenance as the propulsion. Steering systems come in a variety of forms and they essentially comprise three parts: the rudder or steerable drive leg itself, the operating system that connects the rudder to the steering and the steering control. When the drive leg does the steering, such as in a stern drive, and some sail drives and outboard installations, it

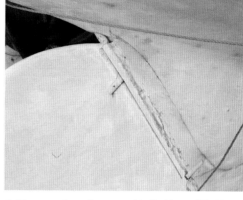

↑ *There are signs of movement in the hinge of that top bearing and also in the stern post.*

replaces the rudder, except perhaps in the case of a sailboat with an outboard where you still need a rudder when sailing. All of these parts are essential to the safe operation of the steering and yet they are often hidden away in the bowels of the boat and may not be easily accessible for inspection.

RUDDER MOUNTS

The simplest form of rudder steering, a transom hung rudder connected to tiller steering, is found on many smaller boats and incorporates all three parts of the steering into one unit. Such an installation is easy to inspect as the components are easily accessible from the outside, but there can still be variations in the way that the rudder is hinged to the transom. Usually there will be a couple of eyes or gudgeons fitted to the transom where the pintles on the rudder engage, so that the rudder is hinged. Here you will be looking for any play in these 'hinges' and while a certain amount of play is permissible, if the holes show any signs of becoming oval or the pintles show wear, it could be time

WHY SURVEY YOUR OWN BOAT?

THE TOOLS OF THE TRADE

THE HULL

DECK AND SUPERSTRUCTURE

ENGINES AND THEIR SYSTEMS

STERN GEAR

PLUMBING

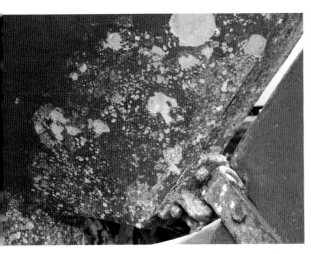

↑ *This rudder bearing needs checking because it does not appear to be seating properly.*

for renewal; once the wear occurs it can quickly accelerate, since there will be more movement in the rudder.

On some smaller motorboats and some sailboats the bottom hinge point of the rudder is often formed by an extension bar running below the propeller and this type of bearing can be more prone to wear because abrasive grit can settle into the socket with no easy means of escape. If

there isn't a drain hole in the bottom it can be a good idea to drill one, at least creating the possibility for grit to pass through the bearing. Move the rudder to and fro in order to check that the bearings are reasonably in line and that there is some means of securing the rudder in place so that it doesn't lift off the bearings in a seaway. This securing may be a nut and lock nut on the bottom of the pintle or it can be a simple split pin through the pintle with a washer between the pin and the socket. To prevent the rudder lifting, some installations rely on the unsatisfactory arrangement of a tiller arm working in a slot through the transom near the deck level; check for signs of wear on the wood or moulding where the tiller arm rubs as the rudder is lifted.

The tiller arm should be tightly fitted to the top of the rudder because, again, any play here will lead to escalating wear and tear. Tiller arms have been known to break off at sea and this is much more likely to happen in rough seas where the strain on the steering increases. A firmly

↓ *Apart from the corrosion, the hole in this rudder support is worn off centre.*

→ *This rudder is only supported by two thin plates so it needs a detailed check.*

↑ Check for play between the tiller and the rudder stock.

second support bearing at the top of the tube and if this is inside the hull, this top bearing will also incorporate a gland to prevent water getting into the hull. If the rudder stock extends up to deck level, it is likely there will be a tiller attached to the top which makes for a relatively simple installation and one in which there is little chance of water entering the hull.

With any type of spade rudder check the system for wear in the bearings by trying to move the rudder from side to side across the boat and then in a fore and aft direction. A small amount of movement is permissible, but if you do find any

bolted connection between the tiller and the rudder head is better than a socket arrangement because then there should be no play in the connection.

So that it doesn't take up room in the cockpit when not in use, on some installations the tiller arm may be hinged at the point where it connects with the top of the rudder to allow for upwards movement; again, check this hinge for wear.

The spade rudder system, where part of the rudder blade is forward of the hinge point to help reduce loading on the steering, is found on many boats, both motor and sail. In this system the bottom of the rudder is unsupported, so that there is considerable strain on the bearings located at the top of the rudder stock. The rudder stock, which on modern boats is usually constructed from stainless steel, enters a tube fixed into the hull; it will have a bearing at the point where it enters the hull and another one higher up. Depending on whether the steering actuator is inside the hull or up on deck there will be a

← This apparent leak could indicate that there is water inside the rudder laminate.

↓ Corrosion is running down from inside the rudder stock so it needs to be lowered for investigation.

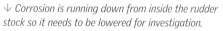

WHY SURVEY YOUR OWN BOAT?

THE TOOLS OF THE TRADE

THE HULL

DECK AND SUPERSTRUCTURE

ENGINES AND THEIR SYSTEMS

STERN GEAR

PLUMBING

↑ *Check for play in the rudder bearings.*

spade rudder can take a lot of punishment and these bearings usually rely on water for lubrication rather than greasing. At one point in the system there will be a support to take the vertical load of the rudder, usually at the top of the rudder stock, where there may also be a grease point for both the bearing and the vertical support. If there is play in the rudder stock and its bearings, the sealing gland at the top of the stock may not seal properly, so check here for signs of leaks.

The tube that provides the supports for the rudder stock may be either metal, and welded or bolted to the hull, or composite, and bonded to the hull. The rudder can be subject to quite high sideways loadings and it is not unknown for the bonding or joint between the tube and the hull to break away and leak. If securing bolts are used they may be subject to corrosion and/or leaks; check closely for any signs of either.

excessive movement, perhaps in the order of 2 or 3mm at the point where the rudder stock enters the bearing, you will need to remove the rudder and check the stock and bearings for wear. The bottom bearing of a

The third type of rudder mounting is where the forward end of the rudder is attached to either a skeg towards the stern

← *This rudder has been lowered so that the stock can be checked.*

↑ *There looks to be some play in the lower rudder bearing support here.*

or directly to the aft end of the keel. You'll mainly find this type of installation on a sailboat and it provides a relatively strong mounting, with the rudder supported at both top and bottom. Such a mounting cannot work with a balanced rudder, although there is a compromise design that has a short skeg with the lower rudder bearing halfway up the rudder and the balanced section below. Once again, check the bearings by trying to move the rudder back and forth in line with the bearing area. Also examine the bottom bearing for any signs of movement and corrosion; cracking in the antifouling paint finish at the joint between the hull and the bearing will indicate movement. It may be just a case of tightening up the securing fastenings, but you may want to go further and remove all fastenings to check for corrosion and wastage.

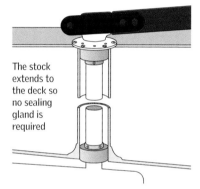

The stock extends to the deck so no sealing gland is required

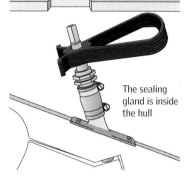

The sealing gland is inside the hull

→ Two types of rudder support.

↓ This leaking oil/grease may just be from over-enthusiastic lubrication of the rudder bearings.

→ Checking the lower edge of the rudder.

WHY SURVEY YOUR OWN BOAT?

THE TOOLS OF THE TRADE

THE HULL

DECK AND SUPERSTRUCTURE

ENGINES AND THEIR SYSTEMS

STERN GEAR

PLUMBING

RUDDER CONSTRUCTION

Rudders are constructed in a variety of ways, from metal plates to wooden fabrications and moulded composites. Steel plates welded to the rudder stock are found on smaller craft. A more sophisticated form may include two shaped steel plates formed into an aerofoil section. Whichever the construction, you're looking for corrosion in the steel. Cast bronze rudders may be used on fast motorboats and while corrosion is not likely to be a problem here, you might see cavitation erosion caused by the bubbles coming off the propeller front. A small amount of erosion of this type is acceptable, but in severe cases the rudder will need building up or replacing and you may also want to examine the propeller for the same cavitation erosion.

Rudders

☐ Are the bearings free of up and down play?
☐ Are the bearings free of sideways play?
☐ Does the rudder blade have integrity?
☐ Is the bottom of the rudder blade free of damage?
☐ Is the rudder stock free of signs of leaking?
☐ Have you checked the anode (in a metal rudder)?
☐ Are the pintle bearings free of wear?
☐ Have you checked the vertical security of the rudder?

SURVEY CHECKLIST

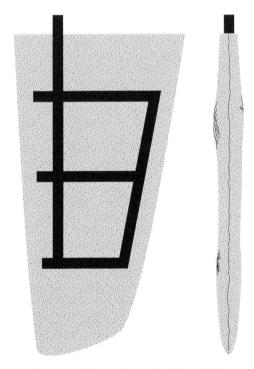

↑ *A laminate rudder may have a steel frame inside. It should be inspected for any swelling, as shown on the right, which may indicate corrosion of the frame.*

Wooden rudder blades are more likely to be found on smaller craft or traditional designs. The wood is supported by metal strips across the grain of the wood and bolted through. This metal may be mild steel, in which case you'll be looking for signs of corrosion, particularly around the securing bolts. Composite rudders tend to be moulded around a foam core to create an aerofoil shape and because the rudder tends to be made in two halves, you want to inspect the joint carefully to ensure they are not coming apart. Have a close look at the bottom of the rudder because this is where damage can occur and water can get into the core material, particularly after a grounding.

Steering operating systems

STEERING OPERATING SYSTEMS can vary as much as the type of rudder and again they are largely out of sight, so you'll need to find access to check them out.

HYDRAULIC SYSTEMS

Many modern boats use hydraulic steering, some of it power assisted. Here the pipes connect and translate the wheel movements into movements of a hydraulic ram attached to the tiller head, which then moves the rudder. Check the piping for leaks by rubbing with your hand to see if there is oil on the outside. Ensure that there is full movement of the rudder from side to side and also check the links and connection around the tiller arm for tightness and security. An autopilot may

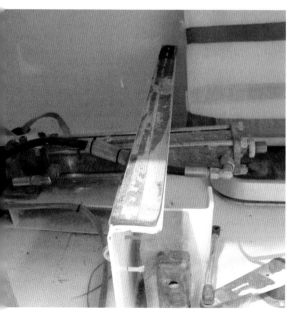

↑ All of the bearings and in this case the hydraulics of the steering system need examination.

be connected into the system, so check the fastenings for tightness. If you turn the wheel and you feel a sort of lumpiness or hesitation in the movement it usually means that there is air in the hydraulics, which needs bleeding off (instructions for this can be found in the boat's handbook).

PUSH PULL CABLES

Push pull cables may be used on smaller craft and on outboard and stern drive installations. Here, you can only really check the system for smooth running and inspect the cables to ensure that they have a smooth path free of sharp bends or kinks. Feel free to examine the connections at each end, although these are normally spring loaded ball and socket joints that shouldn't require maintenance.

WIRE AND PULLEY SYSTEMS

The older wire and pulley steering system was a constant source of trouble; wires would regularly part, or fraying and badly stowed equipment could jam the system. If the boat you're surveying incorporates this system, pull on a pair of leather gloves and run your hand along the wires, feeling for snags.

More sophisticated wire and pulley systems are used to connect the wheel with the tiller arm of sailboats and here a quadrant is fitted to the top of the rudder stock with the wires running in grooves around this. Pulley systems guide the wires on the usually short run from the wheel to the quadrant, so check pulleys are free running and wires have good tension and are free of snags. Look for worn wires around the quadrant; any slack here could lead to them coming off and around the pulleys.

WHY SURVEY YOUR OWN BOAT?

THE TOOLS OF THE TRADE

THE HULL

DECK AND SUPERSTRUCTURE

ENGINES AND THEIR SYSTEMS

STERN GEAR

PLUMBING

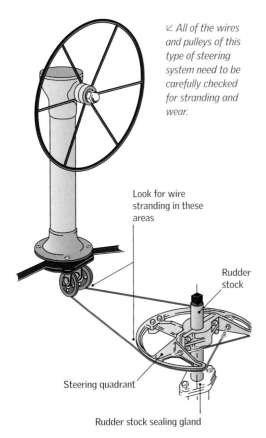

↙ All of the wires and pulleys of this type of steering system need to be carefully checked for stranding and wear.

Look for wire stranding in these areas

Rudder stock

Steering quadrant

Rudder stock sealing gland

SHAFT AND GEAR SYSTEMS

Various shaft and gear systems have been used in the past to translate wheel movements into tiller commands and these are generally self-contained and sealed. Therefore, look for leaks around the gearboxes and for signs of anything rubbing against the shaft sections. As with all steering systems, check that there is only slight play between the wheel and rudder movements, which usually means jamming the rudder in the hard over position first. In a good system there should be no more than a couple of centimetres of movement at the rim of the wheel, although more is acceptable in a wire and pulley system.

Additional underwater fittings

ONCE YOU HAVE checked the propulsion and steering systems – the two main underwater systems on any boat – it's time to move on to the additional underwater fittings.

FLAPS

Flaps, usually stainless steel or cast aluminium plates hinged at the bottom of the transom and extending aft, are found on planing powerboats. Move the flap up and down in order to detect any play in the hinges. Flaps are usually operated by self-contained hydraulic rams and these need to be examined for signs of leakage – check the entire system, both inside and outside the boat. As these rams are underwater when the boat is not being used they need to be fully marinised, so any corrosion here should be viewed with suspicion. You will often find that an anode is attached to the topside of the flap as this keeps it out of the water flow at speed, while maintaining its effectiveness when stopped. Be sure to check for any electrolytic corrosion in the form of pitting.

BOW THRUSTERS

Bow thrusters are found in cross hull tubes set into the front of the hull, so here marine growth is your main problem, especially if the boat has been static in the water for some time. You should be able to turn the impeller by hand and

→ *Flaps on planing powerboats need to have all the moving parts and the hydraulics checked.*

when you do this, check for any play in the drive system (you're unlikely to be able to turn the hydraulically powered thrusters on larger yachts by hand, although they are less vulnerable to corrosion). Smaller boats will have an electrically powered bow thruster, where the electric motor is located down in the bilges of the bow. Again, it may be a case of out of sight, out of mind, so carefully examine the electrical connections and the outside of the motor for corrosion.

ADDITIONAL BOTTOM FITTINGS
Engine water intakes, usually a flanged opening with a grill over the intake, are found towards the rear of the hull. Barnacles and marine growth can build up on the grill if the boat is left afloat and unused for some time, so you'll need to clear it to ensure a good flow of water into the cooling system. Other bottom fittings such as log impellers or sounder transducers should also be free from

growth. Since they are through-hull fittings you'll also need to check inside the hull for any signs of leakage, as any failure here could sink the boat.

Steering
- ☐ Is the system free of play?
- ☐ Are the hydraulics sound with no leaks?
- ☐ Are the wires intact on wire cable steering?
- ☐ Do the guide pulleys run freely with the wire?
- ☐ Are the bearings and connections all tight?
- ☐ Can you get access for maintenance?

SURVEY CHECKLIST

WHY SURVEY YOUR OWN BOAT?

THE TOOLS OF THE TRADE

THE HULL

DECK AND SUPERSTRUCTURE

ENGINES AND THEIR SYSTEMS

STERN GEAR

PLUMBING

7 PLUMBING

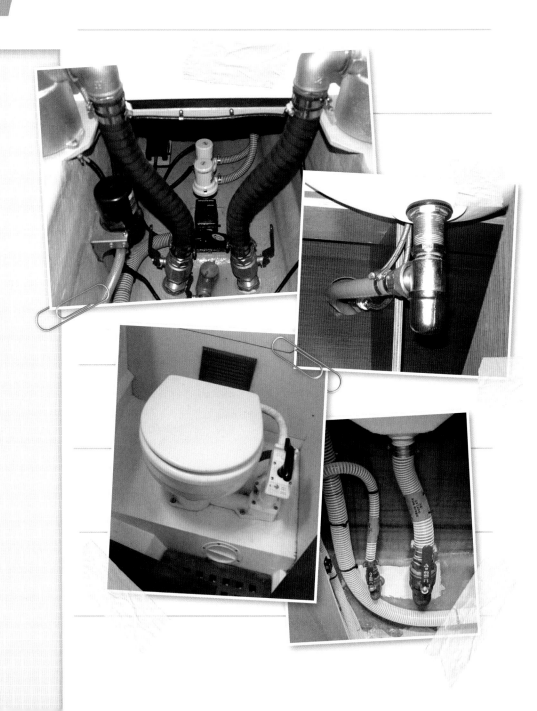

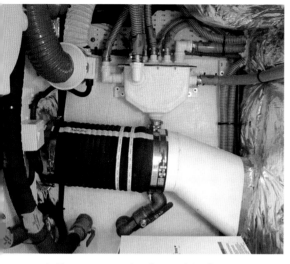
↑ There are many pipes for a variety of purposes on a modern boat and each one needs to be the right material.

↑ The rust stains from this drainpipe need investigating from the inside because they suggest pipe corrosion.

THERE CAN BE a whole range of plumbing inside a modern boat, from the engine cooling system (see chapter 5), to domestic fresh water and toilet supplies; flushing, fire-fighting and bilge pumping systems; drains; and anchor wash, so that if you dig around under the floors and in the bilges you're likely to find pipes of every description. Smaller and older boats may not be so well endowed, but you'll still perhaps see pipes for a cold water supply and bilge pumps tucked away, mostly out of sight and possibly out of mind. Even the smallest boat should have pipework for a bilge pump at the very least.

It can add up to a lot of pipework, and leaks or failures could lead to water in the bilges, corrosion of fittings and, in a worst-case scenario, the boat sinking. So, the first thing you need to do when surveying a boat's plumbing is to differentiate between those parts of the system that are critical to safety, which obviously need a very

careful check, and those which will lead to mere inconvenience or nasty smells if something goes wrong. Some systems are connected to the outside sea by means of through-hull fittings, and these are perhaps the most critical to check during any survey; just because a hull fitting is above the waterline when the boat is at rest, it doesn't mean the hull is immune from flooding if there is a failure here.

Ideally, you'd want to check the entire plumbing system, but you may struggle to access many parts of the system without serious dismantling since it is usually installed before the deck or inner mouldings. Even critical fittings such as the seacocks, which you may need to find and operate in a hurry if a pipe or joint fails at sea, can be hidden from view. Add incoming water and a submerged seacock and you can see how panic might set in quickly! Therefore if you can, try to get hold of the plumbing system for the boat, which makes it easier to trace

WHY SURVEY YOUR OWN BOAT?

THE TOOLS OF THE TRADE

THE HULL

DECK AND SUPERSTRUCTURE

ENGINES AND THEIR SYSTEMS

STERN GEAR

PLUMBING

↑ Some of the plumbing for a toilet system.

the various pipes. If you're surveying your own boat, label the pipes as you discover what they do and where they lead.

Fresh water systems

THE FRESH WATER system usually comprises a tank, a pump and the piping to the taps/showers. On more sophisticated installations you may also find a separate hot water system connected to the engine via a heat exchanger or calorifier, in which engine heat is used to heat the domestic water. Alternatively an electric immersion heater may be present or, more rarely, a diesel-fired heater.

Modern yachts have quite sophisticated systems for supplying all the bathrooms and the galley, while on older boats there may be just one or two outlets in the galley and the toilet compartment. The pump that circulates the water may be hand or electrically operated and here all you can do is a visual check for corrosion, although

you may be able to test that the pump is working.

The best material for pipework is PVC because not only does it stand up well to vibration, it is easy to install and does not corrode. The same copper found in land systems is sometimes used, which isn't ideal because it doesn't stand up well to vibrations. Polyurethane flexible piping is the easiest to install, but this can harden over time and may crack with age.

Any problems are likely to be found in the pipework, so check that it is adequately secured in place (unsecured pipes could cause trouble when the boat is at sea) and free of leaks (in copper piping, leaks show in the tell-tale green signs of corrosion). Also check that the tank, which can be quite a weight, is securely fastened if it is a stand-alone unit. Any signs of movement will be evident in chafe or wear at the same securing points as the fuel tank (see chapter 5).

↓ There should be access to the bilge pump suction in case it gets blocked.

The fresh water system pumps water into a sink, wash basin or the shower tray, but it of course has to drain away after use. Water may drain into a grey water tank and then be pumped overboard or there may be a direct drain. The pipework for such a drainage system is not particularly critical except of course that the pipe eventually connects with an overboard drain, meaning it can be open to the sea. Therefore it should meet the highest standards and be secured with clips on the flexible sections and the outlet fitted with a seacock (many boats don't have the seacock on the basis that it is only a drain, but that is a false economy if the internal pipe gives way).

The thing with the fresh water system is that any failure is not usually critical to the safety of the boat; at worst it may pump out water from the tank into the bilges, but the only outside connection to the hull is the filling pipe for the tank.

↑ *The U-bend from a sink in the accommodation.*

↓ *Pipework, including the engine exhaust, which is running unsecured in the bilge.*

↓ *Flexible water supply pipework lying loose in the bilge.*

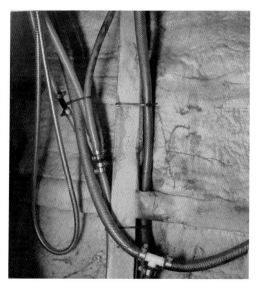

Toilet systems

THE TOILET SYSTEM is much more critical both as far as the safety of the boat is concerned and your comfort on board. However, it is yet another difficult system to examine in detail: today's modern systems are usually supplied as a complete system to ensure reliability, but on older toilets you'll usually need to poke around behind or below the toilet to get access to the pipework. For a full check it would probably be necessary to remove the toilet completely.

WHY SURVEY YOUR OWN BOAT?

THE TOOLS OF THE TRADE

THE HULL

DECK AND SUPERSTRUCTURE

ENGINES AND THEIR SYSTEMS

STERN GEAR

PLUMBING

Systems can vary considerably in terms of installation and sophistication, with the old – and basic – system being a toilet bowl with a pump that sucks water in from outside before the mix in the bowl is pumped out overboard. These toilets are usually installed at or below the waterline, so the integrity of the water systems is vital since a failure can let water into the boat.

The inlet pipe – a small diameter flexible pipe connecting a seacock to the toilet pump – is usually fitted at a lower level than the exit pipe. The exit pipe is larger in diameter to allow solids to pass through, and the usual exit for this pipe is just below the waterline when the boat is upright. Again, a seacock is fitted at the outlet. We will take a closer look at seacocks later in the chapter, but for now check that high quality piping is used for the whole installation and it is secured at each connection by double worm drive hose clips (it may be good practice to close these toilet seacocks when at sea, since there are higher stresses on the pipework when the boat is pounding into waves, but then, of course, the toilet is out of action).

The type of flexible piping used is

↑ *On board toilet systems need reliable pipework to ensure that they work properly.*

also important and at the very least this should be wire reinforced plastic, and the plastic should be of a grade that does not harden with age, which would create the possibility of cracking. If you're surveying your own boat, it would be worth replacing the hose, say, every five years.

These days you are only allowed a direct discharge of sewerage into the water when well out at sea and most modern systems and many older ones have had to be upgraded to a system that features a holding tank. Such a tank allows for the sewerage to be held on board when

↓ *Alternative toilet systems.*

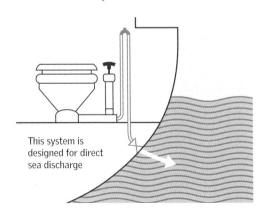

This system is designed for direct sea discharge

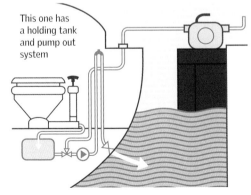

This one has a holding tank and pump out system

WHY SURVEY YOUR OWN BOAT?

THE TOOLS OF THE TRADE

THE HULL

DECK AND SUPERSTRUCTURE

ENGINES AND THEIR SYSTEMS

STERN GEAR

PLUMBING

in the marina or in harbour, before it can be pumped out at sea or at one of the dedicated pump-out stations now found in most marinas. Such a system is more complex and involves having a pump and/or macerator in the system to break up the solids when pumping out. These holding tank systems generally use rigid PVC piping for the outflow from the toilet to the tank, and here again you're looking for any signs of leaks. The pipe from the pump to the overboard outlet is likely to be flexible and is first routed upwards before turning downwards to the skin fitted with a suction break valve at the top, which prevents water siphoning back into the tank from outside. Many modern boats have electric or vacuum toilets that are designed to use the minimum amount of water, so that the black water holding tank does not fill up rapidly. They usually use fresh water, so at least here you only have one through-hull fitting to examine. Any problems in the toilet system can usually be detected initially by the smell, but don't wait for that before doing your checks.

Drainage systems

THE DRAINS THAT take water from spray, rain or washing down overboard will also have an overboard discharge, and this should have a seacock fitted. Furthermore, many modern boats do not allow any through-hull fittings in the topsides so they have to exit underwater. The most obvious drains are those found in sailboat cockpits and these often have crossover piping so that water does not flow back up the pipe when the boat is heeled under sail. This means that the port

drain will exit on the starboard side and vice versa. Again, because these drains are connected to the outside sea the piping needs to be reinforced and of the best quality, and of course a seacock is required.

Deck hatches giving access to the engine compartments, such as those in the cockpit of a motorboat, often have channels fitted outside the hatch seals so that any water collecting here can be drained away and does not find its way below. You may also find drains on the flybridge of a cruiser so that water is collected and drained away below the waterline, meaning it won't stain the pristine topsides. These various drains are often channelled into one collector and, from there, a pipe leading first to a seacock and then overboard.

For preventing leaks below and sea water entering the hull, there is really no substitute for high quality in such drainage systems and on the final pipe overboard. All pipework should also be secured against movement in order to reduce the chance of the plastic sections of the pipework cracking with age. If you can, perform a water test which will indicate any leakage.

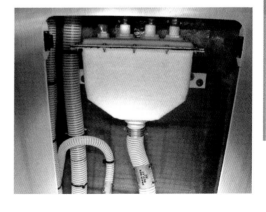

↓ A collection box for various cockpit drains reduces the need for overboard discharges pipes.

Anchor and deck wash systems

ANCHOR WASH SYSTEMS are a modern development designed to keep any mud that comes up on the anchor chain off the deck, so that the chain is washed clean in the anchor locker. Of course, such a system doesn't stop some of the mud dropping off as it comes across the deck and into the capstan, but at least it does not wash down the deck. Anchor and deck wash systems can draw in sea water with a pump and distribute it where required. The wash system is essentially a nozzle (or nozzles) that squirts water onto the chain as it drops into the chain locker, so it is largely out of sight. Drains are fitted at the bottom of the locker, usually just above the waterline so that the water/mud mixture can drain away automatically. The whole system is designed to be automatic: just press a switch to start the pump and the water does the rest. A deck wash system works in a similar way and the two may even be combined with a valve to switch the water flow from one to the other.

Once again, here is a system that requires a high quality installation. First you have a suction inlet where the water is drawn in, so any failure here will allow water into the boat. Second, if the delivery hose is leaking, water is being pumped into the boat, possibly into places without an outlet. Once again it is a question of double worm drive clips on the hoses and high quality hoses to ensure reliability and security. You'll also need to check the outlet drains at the bottom of the chain locker; they need to be clear and large enough to drain the debris coming off the chain. The switch that controls the anchor wash pump will often be found on the dashboard where it could get knocked on accidentally and if the drains are not clear, the chain locker can fill with water and the weight can force the boat to start going down by the head.

Bilge pumps

BILGE PUMPS ARE an essential part of the boat's equipment and you will usually find one in each compartment when the compartments are isolated and do not drain into a common sump aft or amidships. You can get both hand operated and electric bilge pumps, with the latter being an almost universal fit except on the smallest of boats. As they are designed for a one-way flow taking water out of the boat, there should not be any major problems here. However, bilge pumps tend to be out of sight, out of mind, so during a survey, try introducing some water into the bilges to check they are actually functioning. With the boat up on dry land you might want to check there's nobody standing under the outlet before you do this!

Apart from the bilge pumps not working in their automatic mode the only other problem you might find with this system is that the hose on the discharge side is coming adrift or isn't adequately secured, so that any water pumped from the bilge promptly returns there. This won't be much help if one of the other pipes on board has failed during an emergency.

Electric bilge pumps are usually wired to the boat's battery so that the connection bypasses the main battery switch in order to allow the pump to continue working when the boat is unattended. Therefore, check that this wiring and its connections are to the highest standards so that failure is not an option.

Hoses

THE QUALITY OF the hoses used for the various systems on board is vital to ensure safety. You may find around ten different types of hose on board a boat, including the specialised types used for fresh water, sanitation, propane, engine exhausts, pump suction, fuel, hydraulics

and engine cooling water. It is essential that when checking hoses you ensure they are of the right quality for the particular application. Of course, it's not always easy to identify whether a hose is of the right type just by looking at it, but most hoses have some sort of reinforcement material incorporated into their make-up, usually a steel spiral, synthetic textile or combination of the two, and this may give you a clue about the quality. The steel spirals are found on exhaust hoses, some fuel pipes and those required for sanitation and suction. The steel spiral will often be combined with a synthetic fabric reinforcement.

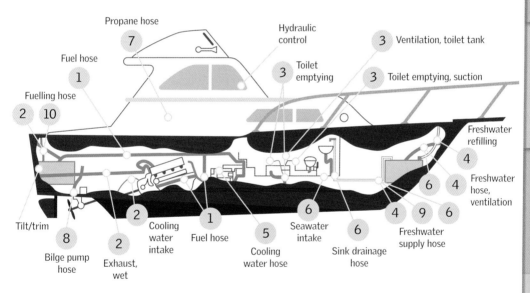

↑↓ Various types of pipe for boat systems and where they might be located within a boat.

WHY SURVEY YOUR OWN BOAT?

THE TOOLS OF THE TRADE

THE HULL

DECK AND SUPERSTRUCTURE

ENGINES AND THEIR SYSTEMS

STERN GEAR

PLUMBING

Hoses

SURVEY CHECKLIST

- ☐ Is the correct type of hose used?
- ☐ Are there any signs of leaks?
- ☐ Are adequate hose clips used?
- ☐ Are the hose clips free of corrosion?
- ☐ Are hoses free of any sign of swelling?
- ☐ Are hoses free of any signs of deterioration?

↑ *Engine water intakes with seacocks and bilge pump piping.*

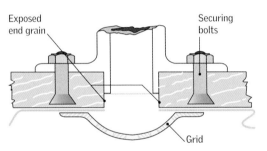

Exposed end grain

Securing bolts

Grid

↑ *This is how a skin fitting might be secured in the hull. The exposed laminate or wood ends would need to be sealed off.*

↓ *Skin fitting and pipes associated with bathroom fixtures.*

While you may not be able to assess the quality of hoses that are in place during the survey, at least you can ensure the correct type of hose is used when any replacement is carried out. You may see cheaper hose alternatives in use, but there is no substitute for good quality hose when you're trying to avoid an unnecessary risk of failure. Check for corrosion, leaks and swelling and make a note to replace any that fall below the required quality.

Seacocks

NOW WE COME to the seacocks, which could be considered the safety net for all of these systems taking water from outside the hull into the boat or allowing water to drain overboard. There are a surprising number of these inlets on any boat, especially when you include the engine connections too, and most of these connections should incorporate a seacock so that the hole in the hull can be closed off if there is any problem with the internal system. You will find that exceptions can

WHY SURVEY YOUR OWN BOAT?

THE TOOLS OF THE TRADE

THE HULL

DECK AND SUPERSTRUCTURE

ENGINES AND THEIR SYSTEMS

STERN GEAR

PLUMBING

be made on those pipes or systems in which the outlet is above the waterline, but if a boat is operating in rough seas or it is a sailboat that will heel over, those above-water outlets can find themselves submerged (the only pipe that doesn't have a seacock fitted is the engine exhaust pipe).

Having a seacock fitted is one thing but that seacock won't be much use if a) it is not in working order and b) it is not easily accessible.

Good quality seacocks are made from non-corroding bronze and comprise a plate (the attachment point to the hull), the valve itself and its operating lever/handle, and a spigot (the attachment point for the hose). The attachment plate usually sits on the inside of the hull with the attachment bolts passing through the hull. There may be a wooden pad between the seacock plate and the hull to help spread the local loading, while there should be a spigot that extends from the plate to the outside of the hull to help seal the cut edges of the hull laminate or planking. This is important, as it prevents

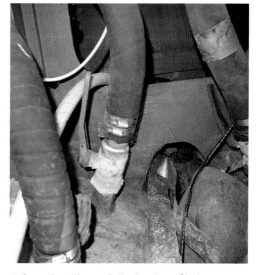

↑ *Seacocks with very distinctive signs of leakage.*

water from entering the exposed internals of the laminate or wood, which could set off delamination or rot in the exposed sections. A grille is usually fitted outside when the pipe is an inlet in order to reduce the chance of solid matter entering the seacock and blocking the pipe. On metal hulls the seacock may be bolted or even welded directly onto the metal plating. In aluminium hulls, stainless steel seacocks may be specified to reduce the chance of electrolytic corrosion.

SEACOCK TYPES

There are three main types of seacock: the gate valve, the ball valve and the tapered valve. The gate valve makes its seal with a vertical plate that moves up and down inside the valve. It is controlled by a screw handle so it may require several turns to open and shut the valve.

On modern boats, it is the ball valve that is widely used and this requires just a quarter of a turn on the operating lever to open or close the valve, which makes

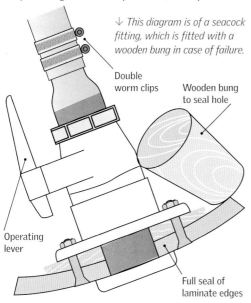

↓ *This diagram is of a seacock fitting, which is fitted with a wooden bung in case of failure.*

Double worm clips

Wooden bung to seal hole

Operating lever

Full seal of laminate edges

operation quick and simplifies things in an emergency. Here there are seals inside the valve to ensure the whole thing is watertight when closed.

More likely to be found on older boats, the tapered valve is similar in its operating lever system, requiring just the quarter turn to operate it, but here the moveable part of the valve is a tapered cone that operates inside a matching tapered hole. The adjustment in the valve may require tightening to form the seal in the moveable tapered part. Tapered valves may require stripping down every so often in order to grease the moving and fixed parts and to reset the valve adjustment, or the adjustment may be spring loaded to draw the taper in tightly to its seating.

↑ This seacock has a connecting hose, which has only one worm drive securing clip. When the handle is up the seacock is closed.

↓ A similar seacock with earthing wires to reduce the chance of electrolytic corrosion.

Seacock condition is a bit like a barometer for the condition of the rest of the boat, both in the original standard of construction and the level of maintenance that has taken place since the boat was new. The seacock that doesn't need maintenance has not yet been invented: all seacocks need regular maintenance, even if that only means opening and closing the valve a few times and perhaps lubricating it to ensure it works. It is quite easy to see whether a seacock has been operated in this way because the handle will be clean and shiny and there should be no signs of corrosion.

However, the chances are you'll find the seacocks in a neglected condition during your inspection and in this case you'd need to examine them a lot more closely. It is not unusual to find evidence of corrosion on the outside, and if you struggle to operate the valve by hand, it will need stripping down to free things up. If you see salt crystals around the seacock, it is probably leaking. Any signs of neglect should raise alarm bells: chances are, if the valve hasn't been properly maintained or operated regularly, the attached pipework and securing clips may have suffered from comparable neglect. Any through-hull seacock should have at least double worm drive clips securing the flexible pipe to it and any signs of swelling in the rubber or plastic at the attachment point should be a warning sign that replacement is required. Pipework should also be checked for surface cracking, which can indicate ageing. Again, you may find that the seacocks on the engine cooling water intakes show signs of having been maintained or at least operated, since they are reasonably accessible, but those

← There are distinct signs of leakage around this seacock.

Plastic will generally harden after ten years or more, particularly where it is exposed to sunlight, so fittings of this type should be viewed with a degree of caution on older boats where they may have become brittle; if they have turned yellow, it might be a good idea to replace them. Plastic fittings of this type are not recommended at or below the waterline where every connection should have a metal seacock built in.

tucked away in other less accessible parts of the boat may have been neglected.

On above water outlets you will often find skin fittings made from plastic that simply have a contoured outside flange held tightly in place with a washer and nut in matching material on the inside. It's a simple solution to providing a pipe outlet and it can work for bilge pump and similar outlets that are mounted well above the waterline. These skin fittings do not have a seacock incorporated into the system and they are simply a termination to the pipe.

Because of their importance to the safety and security of the boat, you would think that seacocks would have been designed to be more accessible in case of emergency. Even the various authorities don't seem to be concerned with accessibility, only requiring that seacocks are fitted to underwater inlets and outlets. Some form of external or extension means of operation would certainly help, since in the event of a failure of any of these systems, the operating lever of the seacock is likely to be the first thing that goes underwater.

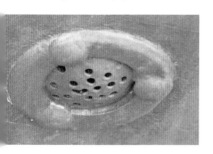

← The outside of a water intake. It is important to check that the holes are kept clear.

↓ The skin fitting where a depth sounder normally fits but is temporarily used for the water hose intake.

Seacocks

SURVEY CHECKLIST

- ☐ Is the lever or wheel operation accessible?
- ☐ Is the lever or wheel operation working freely?
- ☐ Are valves and pipework free of signs of leaks?
- ☐ Are securing clips in good condition?
- ☐ Are hose connections in good condition?
- ☐ Is the hull mounting sound and free of corrosion?
- ☐ Is the outside grille unclogged?

WHY SURVEY YOUR OWN BOAT?

THE TOOLS OF THE TRADE

THE HULL

DECK AND SUPERSTRUCTURE

ENGINES AND THEIR SYSTEMS

STERN GEAR

PLUMBING

8 MASTS AND RIGGING

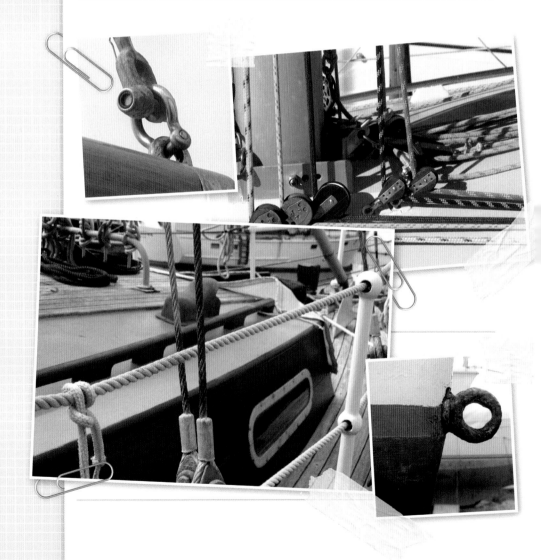

MASTS AND RIGGING

THE ELECTRICAL SYSTEM

THE INTERIOR

SAFETY EQUIPMENT

RIBS AND TENDERS

THE TEN MINUTE SURVEY

AFTER THE SURVEY

← You can view the masthead fitting with binoculars if there is no direct access.

→ All of the detail on the mast fittings should be examined at every opportunity.

THIS CHAPTER IS mainly for the sailboat owner or prospective owner of a boat in which the mast and rigging is a very important part of the structure; however, it also applies to motorboats fitted with a boat launching derrick or fishing boats on which you need to survey the trawling gear or similar equipment.

The rigging of a boat can be quite a complex structure, and there are various options for its set-up, so one of the first things to do during a survey of the mast and rigging is to pin down what system is being used and how it all hangs together.

It can often look very fragile, with thin strands of wire and the seemingly impossibly thin mast supporting the stress and strain of the sails.

The first dilemma you'll face when surveying the mast and rigging is whether to check it with the mast up or down. In some ways you want to have the mast erected to see how the whole system works and to reveal any existing weak points or wear, but it's difficult to do a full check on rigging that is under tension since most of the wear points will be in the 'nip', the point where two fittings, such as

→ Checking the rigging screws is a vital part of any survey.

a shackle or clevis pin, link at the top or bottom of a wire. This can be a particular problem at the masthead fittings; you could examine them with binoculars or even make a trip up the mast in a bosun's chair, but unless the rigging is slack enough so that the links in the system can be opened you won't be able to determine if there is wear here. Therefore, in order to examine the fittings in detail the mast needs to be down. It's unlikely the sails will be erected during a survey, but the mainsail may be on the boom or in the mast with a mast reefing system, and a roller reefing jib could still be in place.

↑ *The mast step has a lot of the electrical wiring passing through it to supply the masthead fittings.*

The mast

MAST INSTALLATION

IF THE MAST is erected, start your survey by studying it closely. Look at how the mast is fitted in the boat. On older boats it may go through the deck with the heel connecting with a mast step just above the keel. The alternative, and the system used on most modern yachts, is to have the mast step on the deck or on the coachroof, which in turn is supported by a tube or column between the coachroof and the keel or bottom framing. This latter arrangement does away with the need to have some sort of seal around the point where the mast passes through the coachroof or deck, which has traditionally always been a source of trouble and leaks: the mast is always going to move slightly under the stresses and strains of sailing and so trying to seal this joint adequately is difficult. The traditional fix was to place mast wedges in the hole around the mast before fitting

a canvas cover over them to keep the water out. A more modern system might employ a rubber boot as the seal, held in place by worm drive clips. In either case look below for signs of leaks, and if there is staining check the condition of the seal. If the seal has been removed you may see signs of movement around the joint where the mast passes through the deck/ coachroof, which will be revealed by shiny areas on an aluminium mast or wear on a wooden mast. This isn't a serious problem (since there is always a certain amount of movement at this point) unless the wear looks considerable.

The mast step, whether it is inside or outside the boat, is a critical part of the installation as it takes the considerable downward stress of the mast and transmits it to the hull structure. There will often be a pad of some sort in the mast step, which acts as a shock absorber. On the rare occasions when the mast is removed, check the mast step and mast heel for cracks or distortion. You may find corrosion at the

MASTS AND
RIGGING

THE ELECTRICAL
SYSTEM

THE
INTERIOR

SAFETY
EQUIPMENT

RIBS AND
TENDERS

THE TEN
MINUTE SURVEY

AFTER THE
SURVEY

↑ The base of the mast can be subject to corrosion if it lies in water.

↑ The mast step takes a lot of stress, as indicated by this fractured base.

base of the mast, since water can lie in this area. If the mast is stepped on deck, the supporting pillar below it will normally be a rigid structure in metal, so check its base for corrosion. To be certain that it is taking the downward strain, use a straight edge to make sure it's not bent or bowed in any way.

MAST TYPES

The mast is a complex structure requiring detailed examination. It is likely to be constructed from wood or aluminium, with carbon fibre composites usually only seen on racing yachts. You'll find many fixtures and fittings attached to the mast in the way of the boom, spreaders, slots for pulleys, lights, antenna(e) and rigging wire attachments. The complication is increased when there is in-mast reefing for the mainsail.

Hollow wooden masts are designed to reduce weight but even here most or all of the attachments and ropes will be on the outside so examination is relatively

↑ The sheaves and other moving parts need inspection when the mast is down.

→ This bend wind indicator may be only the obvious damage at the masthead, but all of the fittings need close inspection.

↑ *There is corrosion in the masthead plate, which is not visible until the mast is taken down.*

↑ *Hidden corrosion where a fitting has been removed from the mast.*

straightforward, provided you can get close access. Check fittings for any sign of movement, such as slight abrasion in the varnish surface or the wood itself. Certain designs may encourage water to collect behind the fitting, which could start to rot, so look for discolouration of the wood. In particular, check the base of a wooden mast if it lies inside rather than on the boat. Close examination of discoloured fittings may require removal.

If you're examining an aluminium mast, you should focus on detecting corrosion. Aluminium is extremely durable but most mast fittings will be made from stainless steel, meaning you have two dissimilar metals in the presence of sea water which could start electrolytic corrosion (seen in the creation of a grey/white powder around the meeting point). The aluminium will suffer more than the stainless steel, although if the latter is low quality you may also see some rust coloured surface corrosion. Fittings are usually fastened to the mast with rivets, which could be a

different type of metal again, so you must check all of them for the same signs of corrosion. Of course, if the mast is erected you will only be able to see the bottom part of the fitting as you look up with your binoculars.

If the mast is still up, stand back from the boat to examine the rigging. This will enable you to detect any fittings that are out of line, which could place them under additional strain. Modern rigging tends to allow for a degree of unevenness via the use of toggles and similar fittings which take up a natural alignment, so that angles are not so critical here. However, be sure to check all fittings closely. You might see this misalignment where a shackle is attached to the chain plates and the span of the shackle opening is much wider than the width of the chain plate to which it is attached, thus allowing the shackle to cant over. A shackle that is canted in this way could be a weak point in the rigging, so all shackles should be moused with wire to prevent the shackle pin unscrewing when the rigging vibrates.

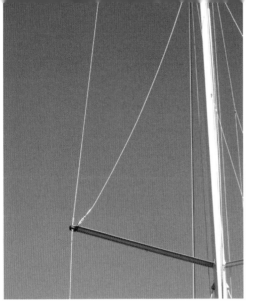

↑ *One of the rigging wires is not doing its job when it is slack.*

↑ *A canted fitting like this can be a weak point. It also generates increased wear.*

There can be a whole collection of fittings at the masthead ranging from halyard blocks to rigging attachments, electronic antenna(e) and navigation lights. These are often out of sight, out of mind so that whenever the mast is taken down, these fittings should be inspected. Binoculars should help you to check that shackles are not coming undone and wires are not unravelling but the detail can only be seen by getting up there or getting the mast down. On a survey you should be looking for any elongation of the holes in lugs where halyard shackles are attached, or in the eyes that may also act as an

↓ *There are numerous fittings on the mast that could cause potential weaknesses.*

MASTS AND RIGGING

THE ELECTRICAL SYSTEM

THE INTERIOR

SAFETY EQUIPMENT

RIBS AND TENDERS

THE TEN MINUTE SURVEY

AFTER THE SURVEY

attachment. Halyard attachments are often slack when the halyard is not in use, which can lead to wear in the holes or in the nip of the fitting.

The boom and its fittings need to come in for a similar check, particularly the gooseneck where the boom attaches to the mast. The double joint here should be checked for wear because it comes under considerable strain. Carefully go over the vang attachments. If the vang is hydraulic check it for any leaks, indicated by a film of oil on the surface. There will be more bits to check on both boats where the sail is reefed into the boom and where there is in-mast reefing. Getting access to the moving parts on these installations can be a challenge and this may be a dismantling job that should be scheduled perhaps every

→ *Many of the fittings for in-mast reefing of the main are hidden inside the mast.*

↑ *The thimble of this shroud connection has been damaged so the wire would also need to be checked for damage.*

↑ *Within this red circle you can see the wear on this pin, which was only discovered when it had been removed.*

↑ *A canted shackle like this can be a weak point.*

MASTS AND RIGGING

THE ELECTRICAL SYSTEM

THE INTERIOR

SAFETY EQUIPMENT

RIBS AND TENDERS

THE TEN MINUTE SURVEY

AFTER THE SURVEY

time the mast is taken out. On a purchase survey inspect everything you can see for the tell-tale signs of wear, such as shiny surfaces and a grey or brown powder.

Mast

SURVEY CHECKLIST

- ☐ Is the mast step secure?
- ☐ Are there signs of movement in the mast step?
- ☐ Are fittings attachments free of corrosion?
- ☐ Are masthead electronics secure?
- ☐ Are the spreaders okay?
- ☐ Are rope guides free and not worn?
- ☐ Is the mast free of bends or bowing?
- ☐ Is the boom gooseneck okay?
- ☐ Are the boom fittings okay?

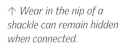

↑ Wear in the nip of a shackle can remain hidden when connected.

↓ The locking nut on this fitting does not appear to have been fully done up.

Standing rigging

CONTACT POINTS ('NIPS')

AS WE SAW earlier in this chapter, the 'nip' is the point at which the two surfaces of an attachment meet. You can't see this contact point until the attachment is slackened off, which enables you to open up the contact points. While everything may look fine from the outside, if a bit of sand or grit gets into the nip and the two surfaces begin to rub together, wear will occur. Where the meeting point consists of two rounded surfaces, the wear will be directly in the nip, while with a tongue and pin fitting (such as might be found on chain plates) the wear will be focused on a pinpoint area. There will always be movement at these points in the rigging, so it's difficult to judge how much of this type of wear is permissible. I'd suggest measuring the diameter of the worn part against the unworn part with a pair of callipers: certainly you should be looking to replace anything more than a quarter of the original dimension, but I would recommend even less because it will only get worse with time.

Every contact point between two parts of the rigging should receive this level of inspection, although you can only really go into this much detail with the mast out of the boat. If you are the boat owner, I'd suggest a bi-annual check along these lines. It might seem extreme, but if one element in the balanced rigging system fails it can start a chain reaction of failure, leading to possible collapse of the mast itself.

RIGGING WIRES

It can be hard to find faults in the rigging wires, so a quick glance is never enough. The first place to look is at the point where the wires terminate in the swages, the securing point for the end of the wire, which in turn are connected to the adjusting rigging screws or connections. The usual arrangement sees a cone fitted inside the swage with its point at the centre of the wire strands. When the swage is tightened up this cone then presses the wire strand against the inner sides of the swage, which locks them into place. There are a number of patented connections but they all tend to work on a similar principle: the point is that you want to examine the point at which the wire enters the swage, since there can be pressure on the wire strands here. Another type of swaged fitting has a stainless steel ferule fitted over the wire and compressed under high pressure around the wire. The ferule was

↓ *Galvanised wire rigging can be prone to corrosion, particularly near connections where there may be dissimilar metals.*

MASTS AND RIGGING

THE ELECTRICAL SYSTEM

THE INTERIOR

SAFETY EQUIPMENT

RIBS AND TENDERS

THE TEN MINUTE SURVEY

AFTER THE SURVEY

under considerable strain when it was fitted and in later life this can make it prone to stress cracking. You may well see signs of corrosion, but you may wish to get out your magnifying glass to get a much closer look at the surface of the fitting.

If there is a bottom connection linking the wire to the rigging screw, the hole where the wire enters is probably not fully sealed, meaning water can lie in the crevices and begin to corrode the metal. Vibration in the wire can aggravate the situation, the outside wires usually being the first to show signs of fatigue. Again, it might be necessary to use a magnifying glass – even if there is only one broken strand, it is a case for replacement of the wire.

Less common are broken strands in the wire along its exposed length, probably caused by historical damage at some time. To check for this deterioration, put on a pair of stout leather gloves and run your hand along the wire to detect any 'snagging' on broken wire ends. Again, replacement is the only solution.

↑ *One corroded strand in this shroud wire suggests poor quality materials.*

↓ *Broken strands where a shroud wire enters the ferule.*

↓ *Fatigue can cause the wires to break at the point where they enter a ferule.*

← A good quality fitting that looks sound but it should be opened up for inspection.

→ Wear in the nip of this stem fitting is evident when it is disconnected.

Both of these checks can be done with the rigging in place so you could use a bosun's chair to get the required access. If you're taking the easy route and using binoculars for a visual inspection, you may be able to see broken strands at the top fixings if the wire has opened up a little, but you'll need to move around to get a view of the wire's full circumference. Certainly in this way you should be able to detect any defects before the wire actually parts, but on a survey a closer inspection is the best solution.

The backstays can be more vulnerable to stranding in this way because they are slackened off when on the lee side, meaning they may be swinging around in the wind. Because of this excessive movement, you must check both the wire at the connections and its securing fitting, such as shackles, for wear in the nip.

The forestay is another vulnerable point: not only does it help to hold the mast up

but it also supports the jib. This support may be in the form of snap hooks that attach the jib to the stay and slide up and down it, but most modern yachts now use a roller reefing system, where the jib rolls up around the forestay fittings. This can add to the stress at the end fittings, particularly the lower one where the operating furling rope connects. The sail also hides the bit that forms the 'tube' around which the sail will roll; this 'tube' should be free to revolve easily as it is turned because if it jams, it can get twisted and may even break, which in turn may tear the sail. The crew can cause this damage to the 'tube' if they're struggling to furl the jammed jib; they take the operating rope to a winch and put excess pressure on the system instead of trying to find the fault. Therefore during a survey the jib, and particularly its swivels and of course the forestay and its hidden connections, should be taken off the furling gear and inspected in detail.

MASTS AND RIGGING

THE ELECTRICAL SYSTEM

THE INTERIOR

SAFETY EQUIPMENT

RIBS AND TENDERS

THE TEN MINUTE SURVEY

AFTER THE SURVEY

↑ It all looks in good condition and secure but furling systems need checking in detail.

↑ This rigging screw is nearing the end of its adjustment.

RIGGING SCREWS

The rigging screws that allow the rigging wires to be adjusted and tensioned can take a lot of abuse, particularly those at the sides which, on top of their intended use of connecting rigging, may also be used for tying off the tender and even mooring ropes. The first thing to look for is any screws that are close to using up their full adjustment – if they are, look for the cause. It may be that the wire to which it is attached was made up too long in the first place or that the wire has stretched, but these are unlikely causes. Perhaps the mast isn't installed in the proper upright position or there is damage in the rigging wire. If both screws on the same side present with this problem, it could be that the mast or possibly even the chain plates are moving. Whatever the issue, do take the time to find the cause because a rigging screw with no more adjustment isn't much use.

Check that the locking devices for the rigging screws are in place. These are usually lock nuts located at the outer ends of the turning part and they are tightened

↓ There is obvious damage to this rigging screw that will weaken it.

121

↑ *No lock nuts on this rigging screw.*

MAST AND CHAIN PLATES

The chain plates and/or the deck fittings to which the rigging screws are attached should also come in for scrutiny. These rigging attachment points are a vital part of the structure: they not only serve to transmit the rigging loads to the hull, but also help to keep the mast where it should be. It is fairly easy to get a look at the external chain plates so check for any signs of movement where they are bolted to the hull, and/or staining of the topsides or paintwork which could indicate that

up against this turning part to stop it moving of its own accord. Since rigging screws can cause chafe on the foresails if they pass outside this point they are often covered in tape or other anti-chafe material, such as a plastic sleeve, so this should be removed to inspect what is happening below. Because of the hard life they lead and their vulnerable position, the threaded section in screws can also become bent, which prevents further adjustment, so check that the threaded sections run true when turned and the rigging screw works throughout its length. This is also the time to look for any wear in the nips of the securing shackles and clevis pins (when the rigging is slackened off, of course).

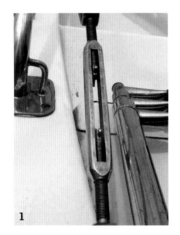

1 *Another rigging screw with no lock nuts to stop it slackening off.*
2 *This rigging screw is nearing the limit of its adjustment.*
3 *This rigging screw has been bent, so is likely to have been weakened.*
4 *The bottom lock nut is not effective here.*

MASTS AND
RIGGING

THE ELECTRICAL
SYSTEM

THE
INTERIOR

SAFETY
EQUIPMENT

RIBS AND
TENDERS

THE TEN
MINUTE SURVEY

AFTER THE
SURVEY

← *The rigging screw and the wire do not line up, which can lead to excessive wear in the nip.*

→ *This chain plate has damaged the gel coat and possibly the laminate underneath.*

bolts on the deck. These are only as good as the laminate they are bolted to, so check for backing pads or plates, tight nuts and for any signs of softness or staining in the laminate: it is not unknown for a rigging attachment to pull out and take part of the deck with it.

there is corrosion beneath, perhaps in the fastening bolts. These bolts should also be checked inside the hull to ensure that they are tight and there is no sign of movement. There should always be a backing plate here to help spread the rigging loadings into the hull structure.

You should get the same backing plates when the chain plates are replaced by deck plates bolted through the deck. Here the loading should be spread between at least the adjacent frames in order to help transmit the loading to the hull structure. Carefully check the deck moulding around the fitting for any signs of softness or staining, which may indicate that water is getting into the moulding around the edge of the fitting or the fixing bolts. At the bow the securing for the forestay is often incorporated into the stem head fitting, while at the stern the backstay(s) may have chain plates bolted to the transom or eye

↑ *Corrosion in this stem fitting could weaken it.*

↑ *The angled pull on this chain plate ring will put excessive strain on it.*

any signs of chafe and wear. Many modern ropes have an outer weave that provides the wear and UV resistance, while the main strength of the rope is in the strands below. If the outer weave gets worn and the inner strands are exposed, it's time for renewal because not only will the wear accelerate but with the outer weave torn the rope could end up jamming in a pulley or clamp. On modern sailboats many of the ropes can take quite a strain when under sail in a blow and this is the last moment that you want one to fail.

Finally, check that the pull of the rigging wire is in line at the tongues fitted to the mast and the chain plates at the bottom of the rigging. It's not unusual to find that there is a misalignment so that there is a sharp change in angle between the rigging and its attachment point, which can place added stress at the point of connection, creating a wear point (you'll need the mast in situ to see this).

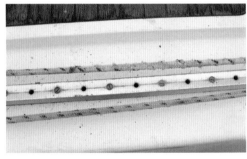

↑ *There can be a considerable strain on the track fittings so the fixings need careful scrutiny.*

↓ *All of the running rigging ropes need to be checked for chafe or other weaknesses.*

Running rigging

RUNNING RIGGINGS ARE the ropes but they may incorporate some wires, such as for parts of the halyards.

ROPES

With so many ropes going up inside the mast it can be difficult to get access to all of them, but if you pull the halyards up and down you'll expose most of the length (although you may need a trip up the mast to see some parts). This is a pretty straightforward check: you're looking for

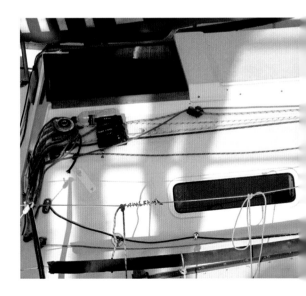

MASTS AND RIGGING

THE ELECTRICAL SYSTEM

THE INTERIOR

SAFETY EQUIPMENT

RIBS AND TENDERS

THE TEN MINUTE SURVEY

AFTER THE SURVEY

↑ *All lead blocks and their attachments need to be examined in detail.*

BLOCKS

While checking the ropes is easy, examining the blocks and leads that they run through can be more of a challenge. The modern system of blocks and ropes is a fascinating cat's cradle that should have been designed for easy sail handling and adjustment. It includes blocks at the top of the mast, which handle the halyards, and at the base of the mast, which lead the halyards out. More blocks are found at the mast base leading the various ropes to the clamps and winches, while finally there are the sheet lead blocks.

You can check most blocks by hand, but for a good check you need the weight off the rope running through the block you're examining, which may be difficult to achieve when looking at the masthead blocks.

Modern blocks are usually made from a combination of stainless steel and tough composites, so they should be corrosion-proof, but they can be subject to wear. If you see wear in a rope it could be a clue that there is wear in the block, since the sheave may not be running true. Try to move the sheave in relation to the frame of the block – there should only be the very minimum of movement between the two, just enough to ensure free running. Any more and it may be time to replace the block. Also look for any signs of the rope rubbing on the sides of the block, which might suggest that there is wear in the sheave bearing or perhaps damage to the pulley itself. While examining the blocks check the securing shackles for wear in the nip and pins (these shackles should be moused).

ROPE CLAMPS

The rope clamps are usually a simple cam operated system and here just a visual check is all that is required to ensure the clamp is operating properly and free of damage. Check the mounting points and fixings, because these clamps can take a heavy strain. Most winches should be stripped down for maintenance and

↑ *This rope clamp has a broken lever so it is ineffective.*

lubrication perhaps once a season, but during a survey you quickly check for wear in the bearings by simply moving the barrel of the winch to and fro. There will always be a small amount of play for the winch to run freely but anything more than a couple of millimetres indicates a more detailed check is required. Finally, examine the mounting fixings as, like the clamps, these can come under heavy strain.

The sails

THE FIRST PLACE to look for signs of wear in the sails would be in the corners and in the pockets for the sail battens, the areas that wear first on a well-used sail. As a general rule a newer sail should feel firm while older sails should have a softer feel, but this is no sure guide. The state of the stitching is another clue to a sail's condition; modern sails are made from a 'harder' fabric than earlier sails, and the stitching tends to sit 'proud' on the fabric surface, leaving it more vulnerable to rapid wear. Check all around the edges of the sail and its attached fittings, such as the mast sliders and the sheet eyes. Be alert to signs of repair, such as inconsistent stitching or patches. If you have any doubts about the durability of a repair, it may be time to call in an expert sailmaker, but keep in mind that he/she may have a vested interest in condemning a sail.

Jibs fitted onto furling systems can deteriorate through UV damage, which is why when the sail is rolled up, the exposed part is often constructed from a coloured material that protects it from harmful rays. This strip can act as a sacrificial part of the sail to be renewed when it deteriorates. UV damage in a more serious form is indicated by a 'powdery' substance on the surface of the sail; by this point, the sail is going rapidly downhill. Any sail fitted to a roller reefing system needs to be checked closely, since these systems can lead to localised chafing if the sail doesn't roll on and off smoothly.

Lifting/hauling systems

IF YOU'RE CHECKING a motorboat with a derrick or boom for boat launching or, on a more serious note, a fishing boat where there are blocks and wires for hauling pots or trawls, these require the same thorough checks. Any failure in a lifting or hauling system can have dire consequences if a heavy load should drop, so take nothing for granted: carefully examine the wires, ropes, blocks and shackles. It is so easy to assume that everything is OK until something in the system fails; the stresses on modern rigs can be surprisingly high, so take nothing for granted.

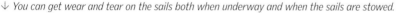
↓ You can get wear and tear on the sails both when underway and when the sails are stowed.

MASTS AND RIGGING

THE ELECTRICAL SYSTEM

THE INTERIOR

SAFETY EQUIPMENT

RIBS AND TENDERS

THE TEN MINUTE SURVEY

AFTER THE SURVEY

9 THE ELECTRICAL SYSTEM

HOW BOATS HAVE changed in the past 30 years. There was a time when the electrical system on a boat would supply the navigation lights, possibly a few interior lights, maybe some electronics and of course the engine starting system. None of this was necessarily vital to the operation of the boat once you got the engine started, whereas today virtually everything on a boat depends on the electrics. Air conditioning, cooking, lighting, sound and television systems are all reliant on electricity; even the engines are electronic, so that they will not run without an electrical supply. We are even moving towards electric motors! In turn the whole attitude towards a boat's electrical system has altered; a casual approach can no longer be tolerated and only the highest standards will do. Any survey of the electrics must determine the quality of the installed systems and any repairs that need to be made to bring them up to scratch.

Batteries

THE PLACE TO start any survey of the electrical system is the battery or, on most modern boats, the batteries. These lie at the heart of the electrical system and if they don't perform, most of the rest of the system won't work. Moreover, the condition of the batteries and their connections can often be a good indicator to the quality of the rest of the electrical system.

The batteries both store the electrical power and supply it on demand; levels of

↑ Batteries in dire need of loving care and attention.

→ Electrical systems are becoming more and more complex on boats. This is a high quality installation.

MASTS AND RIGGING

THE ELECTRICAL SYSTEM

THE INTERIOR

SAFETY EQUIPMENT

RIBS AND TENDERS

THE TEN MINUTE SURVEY

AFTER THE SURVEY

demand can be low and steady or heavy and short, with the latter occurring when the batteries are supplying the engine starter motor or perhaps the bow thruster. A simple system that only supplies the lighting and perhaps, as on a sailboat, the engine starting will usually have just the one battery, but more complex systems may incorporate two or more battery installations, and yet more when a generator has to be supplied with starter power. Therefore, check around the boat to locate the various batteries. You'll usually find them in or near the bottom of the boat, since they are heavy items and the designer generally tries to keep weight low down. While this might be a good plan as far as the centre of gravity is concerned it isn't the best solution for safety; if the batteries are low down in the bilges and the hull starts to flood, you won't be able to make an emergency call as the batteries (and your electricity supply) will be the first thing to go. You can't do much to relocate the batteries but this is a point to bear in mind when assessing the overall suitability of the boat.

SECURE STOWAGE

Wherever the batteries are stowed, they must be secure in their stowage because a battery that can move about, however slightly, can be a cause of future trouble. Apart from potentially damaging the batteries themselves, any movement here can place stress on the connecting wires, usually heavy duty cables designed to carry the high current loads of the engine starter. If they do move, even slightly, the strands of the cable may break or the terminals may become disconnected. Initially, these problems are likely to put pressure on the link to the electrical users, increasing the load on the remaining strands if the wire is fraying or adding to resistance if the battery connection is poor. In either of these scenarios the wire link can heat up and in a worst-case scenario there can be

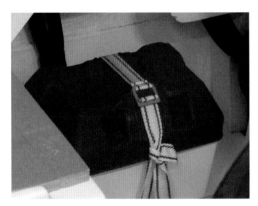

↑ The battery box looks well secured but is the battery secure inside?

→ Webbing straps can come loose. This battery is stowed very close to the cooling water filter.

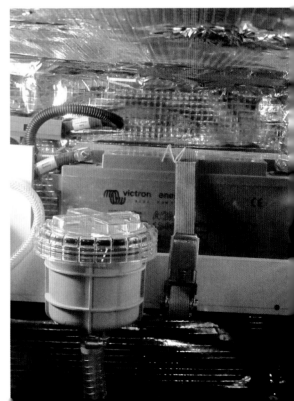

130

↑ *Well-secured batteries in their box.*

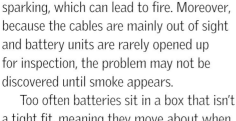

↑ *These batteries are properly stowed and the cables are clamped.*

sparking, which can lead to fire. Moreover, because the cables are mainly out of sight and battery units are rarely opened up for inspection, the problem may not be discovered until smoke appears.

Too often batteries sit in a box that isn't a tight fit, meaning they move about when the boat rolls or pitches. Even wedging them into position in the box may not be enough because wedges can shake loose. The only real way to secure them is through clamping across the tops of the batteries.

Next, check the battery terminals where the main wires connect the batteries to the system. Terminals should be tightly fitted and corrosion free (they are usually constructed from lead to reduce the risk of corrosion from dissimilar connections); they carry a very heavy current for engine starting and any corrosion is likely to cause a resistance to this current and, in a worst-case scenario, it would prevent enough voltage reaching the starter motor even when the battery is well charged. It is normal to grease these terminals in order to reduce the chances of corrosion, but with the current trend towards low or

zero maintenance batteries, they may not receive the attention they deserve.

The heavy duty connecting wires should only have a short unsupported span in order to reduce the chance of any movement in the wire that could cause it to fray or strand in time. This is particularly important on a fast powerboat where there can be considerable pounding in waves.

↑ *These batteries are in a metal clamping system with lock nuts.*

MASTS AND RIGGING

THE ELECTRICAL SYSTEM

THE INTERIOR

SAFETY EQUIPMENT

RIBS AND TENDERS

THE TEN MINUTE SURVEY

AFTER THE SURVEY

131

↑ *Corrosion on battery terminals.*

THE ISOLATION SWITCH
AND HEAVY DUTY CABLES

There should be a battery isolation switch (which allows you to switch off the mains battery supply when the boat is out of use) mounted close to the batteries. This not only reduces the risk of fire but also helps to prevent any power leaks and/or possible

↓ *The main battery isolating switches and their connecting wires.*

electrolytic action on the hull fittings and stern gear. Again, the connections here need careful scrutiny for tightness and corrosion. There may be a connection from the battery that bypasses this isolating switch and this feeds to the electric bilge pump(s) and possibly an alarm system, both of which need to be kept active when the boat is not in use. Because this feed is a direct connection to the batteries, the wire and its connections need careful examination, although bear in mind that the feed may go via a dedicated breaker to isolate the circuit if there is an overload on the wire or pump.

One heavy duty cable extends from the main isolation switch or switches to the starter motor switch on the engine and another, perhaps smaller size cable goes to the main electrical distribution board. Both can carry a heavy current so both the cable itself and its securing needs careful scrutiny because any current leakage here could cause severe sparking and possibly lead to a fire. These cables should be secured at frequent intervals to prevent movement and they should not pass over sharp edges that could cut into the cable insulation. However, when the engine is flexibly mounted there will have to be some movement in the part of the cable that connects to the starter motor, so check for this.

The battery and heavy duty cable installation should be located as close as possible to the starter motor to reduce the chance of cable damage and the possibility of a voltage drop if there is cable resistance. On some sailboats the heavy duty cable might lie loose in the bilges on the run between battery and engine, which

↑ *Wiring in the bilges is never a good solution but at least it is sufficiently secured here.*

MASTS AND RIGGING

THE ELECTRICAL SYSTEM

THE INTERIOR

SAFETY EQUIPMENT

RIBS AND TENDERS

THE TEN MINUTE SURVEY

AFTER THE SURVEY

could be a source of problems and possible danger; it should be secured in place with suitable cable clips.

THE DISTRIBUTION BOARD AND CONNECTIONS

Wires run out from the main distribution board, connecting with the various components of the electrical system. You would think designers would know to place the distribution board somewhere dry, but that's not always the case; I've seen them located beneath the engine hatch, making them susceptible to dripping water if the hatch leaks or when it is opened. This will inevitably lead to trouble (if you can rig up protection, great, otherwise I'd suggest walking away).

You may find that the main distribution board is located in the engine compartment and then perhaps a secondary board in the accommodation. On many sailboats you'll find the domestic distribution behind a panel in the chart space. So often a distribution board will have a panel with switches and breakers mounted on its face with the wiring and connections fitted behind. This means that you can't inspect the connections without unscrewing the panel, but this should be part of any survey where possible since if you're going to find problems, they're likely to be in the connections. Therefore check for any signs of corrosion (a greenish crystalline deposit) in connections and that they are all tightly secured. You'll also find a multitude

133

↑ *The jumble of wires, behind the dashboard, need to be well secured.*

of connections behind the dashboard where there is an array of switches and instruments, and if this dash is in the open, close inspection is once again necessary.

Ideally all connections should be secured by a positive nut or screw system but in practice you'll find they're often just push fit connectors. These should work if they are reasonable quality fittings, and they should be, but sometimes the cheaper components designed for cars are used.

Batteries

- ☐ Are batteries adequately secured?
- ☐ Is there space in battery boxes?
- ☐ Are the heavy duty cables well secured?
- ☐ Are the connections free of corrosion?
- ☐ Are the connections secure?
- ☐ Are there any wires that bypass the main battery switches?

SURVEY CHECKLIST

These are not fit for marine conditions, since they may have dissimilar metals that can allow electrolytic corrosion which will not only produce a poor connection but in time it could eat away at the copper wire and cause the link to fail.

Wiring

AS YOU GO along checking every connection you can access, examine the wiring that links them. On older boats without the complications of high voltage systems, this is likely to be a much simpler proposition. The wiring may not have been installed to the same high standards found on modern boats, but then it is likely to be more accessible for inspection. However, there is also the likelihood that it will have been considerably modified over its lifetime, and here you are likely to find deficiencies because the replacement wiring may have been installed for convenience rather than reliability.

On most modern boats the wiring is installed as a loom, which has been constructed outside the boat and installed and connected as the boat is being built. This should ensure a high standard and reliability, but it does of course mean that much of the wiring will be out of sight and inaccessible. In these circumstances you have to trust the builder to have done a good job and, today, most are fully aware of the need to ensure high reliability in the electrical system. However, check wiring where you can, especially sensitive points where wires pass through a bulkhead or enter a tube or conduit. Lift the wires up to check the areas of insulation at the point of chafing for signs of wear. You could even place additional tape or other materials at the rubbing point to prevent future wear and chafe.

You may also find that the original wiring loom has been supplemented with additional wiring in order to take the supply to equipment fitted after the boat was built. It is tempting to take this additional wiring by the easiest route, which may not be up to the same high standard of the original. You should be able to identify additional wiring as it won't follow the route of the main wiring loom and it may not be adequately secured. Take particular note of any additional wiring that may have been installed to bypass the main distribution boards as this may not have the same breaker and/or fuse protection.

Finally, check all accessible wiring for any signs of melting of the wire insulation, which could be an indication of an earlier short circuit in the wire. The whole length of wire should be replaced if you see melted insulation, since it may also have occurred at other hidden points along the wiring.

↑ Wiring being installed during the building of a boat.

↓ One of these wires has overheated, melting the insulation.

Electrical wiring

SURVEY CHECKLIST

- ☐ Are there signs of melted and/or chafed insulation?
- ☐ Is there corrosion on connections?
- ☐ Is wiring secure against movement?
- ☐ Is wiring protected from water?
- ☐ Are suitable connections used?
- ☐ Are suitable types of wire used?

FUSES AND BREAKERS

Fuses that protect the electrical system break the circuit when there is an overload. This can prevent the wiring itself from becoming overloaded and getting hot and possibly burning out if there is a short circuit in the system. Fuses work fairly reliably in marine use, the disadvantage being that you can quickly run out of them when you are trying to test the circuit and find the fault. Fuses also add to the number of contacts that can corrode, so that on modern boats they have been largely replaced by breakers, a system

MASTS AND RIGGING

THE ELECTRICAL SYSTEM

THE INTERIOR

SAFETY EQUIPMENT

RIBS AND TENDERS

THE TEN MINUTE SURVEY

AFTER THE SURVEY

↑ *From the outside the electrical installation looks fine, but you need to check what is going on behind the panel.*

→ *A wiring installation based around a fuse system.*

that automatically breaks the circuit in the event of an overload. The breaker is a spring loaded device and early breaker systems were not particularly reliable because they could jump out with wave impact. Modern systems are much better, and you only need push the breaker back into position to reconnect the circuit. If it doesn't stay in, there is a circuit fault, so during the survey check that all breakers are on and stay on when each circuit is live. Of course this test does not detect insulation that is about to break down, so a good visual examination of the wiring system is the only real solution.

HIGHER VOLTAGE SYSTEMS

All of the above comments relate to the 12 or 24 volt systems installed on boats, but increasingly modern boats have a generator

or a shore connection that brings higher voltages of 110 or 220 volts AC on board. This 'domestic' type of supply matches that found on shore and enables the installation and running of equipment such as electric cookers and washing machines. While you may now have the comforts of home aboard your boat, these higher voltages can be lethal if there are problems in the electrical systems. All modern installations are consequently fitted with an earth trip that breaks the circuit if there is any sign of electrical leakage, but the wiring also needs to be of the highest standard to ensure safety. It should be of the stranded copper wire rather than the single strand type found in domestic installations on shore because stranded wires are less prone to fatigue breakage if there is movement in the wire. Sockets should only be mounted in dry areas and a damp atmosphere should not be allowed to develop on board when the boat is out of action.

THE GENERATOR

The generator, which supplies on-board power when away from a shore supply, is generally a self-contained unit. These domestic voltage systems have their own distribution board: switch off the system before you open it then check for corrosion and any loose connections. Usually there won't be any outside connections into the higher voltage system except of course in the connection for the shore supply, which is usually plugged in at the transom area. While you can carry out a visual

examination for signs of corrosion, there is little else you can do except to check that the generator has been regularly serviced. If you have any doubts about the condition of a generator, call a service engineer for their opinion.

↑ *The generator is not always installed for easy access in a crowded engine compartment.*

↓ *Here the high and low voltage systems have been separated and the case offers some protection.*

MASTS AND RIGGING

THE ELECTRICAL SYSTEM

THE INTERIOR

SAFETY EQUIPMENT

RIBS AND TENDERS

THE TEN MINUTE SURVEY

AFTER THE SURVEY

↑ *The cable connected to this navigation light is in poor condition.*

OUTSIDE CONNECTIONS ON SAILBOATS

Lower voltage systems will have outside connections in order to take power to navigation lights, deck lighting and perhaps other fittings and fixtures. You'll need to examine the wiring to these fittings closely: a system that was fine when installed can deteriorate with time and use. Moreover, the outside electrical systems on sailboats in particular take a lot of punishment. Port and starboard lights mounted in the bow are directly in the firing line of spray and solid water and may even be underwater in lively seas. Any exposed wiring may also fall foul of the running rigging or sails.

It is usual for the wires on these lights to be taken in through the bottom of the fitting through a watertight gland; there should be a downward loop in the wire before it enters the gland to discourage water from running along the wire and seeping into the fitting. Round cross-section wire is used as this seals better in the gland, but you can often see that the round outer casing of the wire has been pulled out of the gland leaving the two inner wires to make the connection. However, these don't fit the gland opening so water can find its way in. Therefore, examine navigation lights carefully and open up any that look suspect, such as those with poor wiring or perhaps broken glass. Any signs of internal corrosion will mean renewal of the whole fitting. If the boat is your own, this could also be a good time to replace navigation light bulbs, even if they are still working (the last thing you want in a lively sea is to have to change a bulb in the dark).

← *This navigation light has a crazed glass reducing its effectiveness.*

→ *These navigation lights are not mounted according to the legal requirements. The stern light should be much lower.*

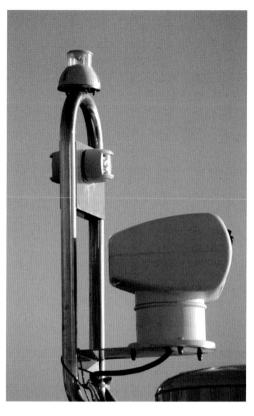

↑ Another example of illegally mounted navigation lights.

removal, but these deck sockets have a hard life. Examine them for any damage caused by people stepping on them or other heavy knocks.

OUTSIDE CONNECTIONS ON MOTORBOATS

The outside electrical fittings on motorboats don't have quite such a hard life as sailboats in most cases, but the same standards of safety should apply. Items such as the horn and searchlight can be exposed to the elements, so scrutinise the exterior for corrosion or leaks. Any external lighting should be mounted in relatively protected areas but it can still be exposed to saltwater, which is one of the most corrosive elements as far as the electrical system is concerned. You'll probably need to replace any fitting showing signs of corrosion.

↓ These navigation lights will not be effective at these angles.

While you can only truly assess the condition of mast lights if the mast is taken down, they are less vulnerable to damage, since they are clear of the running rigging and sails (spreader lights are much the same). Mast light wiring is generally taken down inside the mast where it may have to mix with wiring for the masthead mounted wind instruments, possibly the antenna, and also the halyards, meaning it may not be a happy environment. If you can get access to each end of both the mast and wires (i.e. when the mast is down), test the resistance or voltage drop of the wires.

There should be a deck connection for these internal wires to allow for easy mast

MASTS AND RIGGING

THE ELECTRICAL SYSTEM

THE INTERIOR

SAFETY EQUIPMENT

RIBS AND TENDERS

THE TEN MINUTE SURVEY

AFTER THE SURVEY

The chain locker

THE CHAIN LOCKER houses the motor and control box for the electric capstan, if one is fitted. Capstan manufacturers recognise that their equipment has to operate in extreme conditions, so their equipment is usually built to the highest of standards. However, the actual electrical connections can be the weak point, so you should perform a detailed examination. This can be a case for using a mirror on a stick or a digital camera, since it is a tricky area to access. Once you can see the area, check for corrosion of any sort on the motor or connecting boxes; its presence should be a cause for concern and you should consider a closer inspection (using the mirror on the stick or digital camera method).

In the chain locker there is always the risk of the chain itself causing damage to the capstan motor or wiring if there is a jam in the chain as it goes out, so check that it runs smoothly. Finally, check the seals on the connecting wires where they pass through the bulkhead on their run aft for any signs of deterioration.

The alternator

SO FAR WE have looked at the electrical system from a distribution point of view, but you'll also need to check the alternator on the engine, which supplies the electrical power to keep the batteries charged. We saw in chapter 5 how to check the tension and condition of the alternator drive belt, and if you're surveying your own boat this might be a good time to replace the belt even if there are no obvious signs of wear (on modern engines the drive belt often

↑ *Signs of corrosion starting in the capstan electric motor.*

↓ *The electric cable seals in the bulkhead need to be checked for effectiveness.*

powers the water pumps and other engine systems meaning replacement can be quite a complex task, one that is certainly best done in the quiet of harbour rather than at sea). Since the alternator, and in most cases its connecting wires, are part of the engine system it should have been engineered to the same high standards of the rest of the engine. However, at some point the engine systems have to connect with the boat systems and this is where you need to examine the links to ensure that there are no signs of corrosion or chafing.

The logical place to locate the battery charger, if there's one on board, would be the engine compartment, but they are often located elsewhere, usually around the stern, which allows for easy connection to shore power. Once again, examine the charger unit for deterioration and the connections for any signs or corrosion or damp; depending on the extent of the corrosion, it may need replacing.

AUXILIARY CHARGING SYSTEMS

Many boats today are fitted with auxiliary charging systems that use wind or solar power to keep the batteries topped up. Solar panels are a static system that should not require any maintenance except regular cleaning, but check that the panels are intact and free from damage to the surfaces or the electrical connections. Wind chargers have moving parts and although they are designed to require minimum maintenance, check that there is no play in the shaft, the blades are free of damage and the electrical connections are sound.

The complexity of the modern boat electrical system is enormous, probably beyond the comprehension of the average owner. In most cases, the best you can hope for is that it has been engineered to a high standard and you, as the surveyor, need only check those areas that are visible, since these are the most likely parts of the system to be exposed to a salt or damp atmosphere.

↓ Wind generators and any mast mounted equipment need the wiring checked.

MASTS AND RIGGING

THE ELECTRICAL SYSTEM

THE INTERIOR

SAFETY EQUIPMENT

RIBS AND TENDERS

THE TEN MINUTE SURVEY

AFTER THE SURVEY

10 THE INTERIOR

MASTS AND RIGGING

THE ELECTRICAL SYSTEM

THE INTERIOR

SAFETY EQUIPMENT

RIBS AND TENDERS

THE TEN MINUTE SURVEY

AFTER THE SURVEY

↑ *An example of the shiny interior of a modern boat. You need to look behind the gloss.*

THE INTERIOR OF a modern boat is designed to impress and the inner workings are usually hidden from view and tucked away so that your boat looks like a home from home. It is hard to imagine discovering any problems in this area during a survey because all you are seeing is the glossy interior that is designed to hide the realities of operating a boat. This is particularly the case with modern motorboats but the trend is extending into modern sailboats, too, but in fact the interior is often where you'll find many clues regarding the general boat structure and fittings. For that reason, you're much more likely to find interior problems on older boats, but their workings tend to be much more apparent and accessible, making it a lot easier to poke around and find the trouble spots.

Certainly some of the problems that may affect the interior of a yacht have already been covered in other chapters of this book, since they relate to the on-board systems or to problems that have originated outside, but there are some exterior problems that will only show up on the interior. Leaks through fittings attached to the deck are much more likely to be apparent on the inside than on the outside and problems with electrical wiring or plumbing will be inside the boat. Therefore surveying the interior requires a more holistic approach, since you'll be examining a variety of areas and systems.

↓ *Where is any water in the bilges coming from?*

→ *There are signs that the step covering is lifting and this would need to be inspected.*

To start a survey of the interior you want to remove as much of the covering as possible. Start with the easy bits: remove cushions, bedding and drawers and open covers, which should at least allow you some access to the less visible parts of the interior. For everything else, wait until you see evidence of a problem before going into large scale removal of fixed parts. For

↑ *Open up the boat as much as possible to explore the hidden depths.*

→ *Stains in the bilges need to be investigated.*

↑ *The autopilot compass is found hidden away in a locker.*

example, if you see signs of staining on the deck head lining, you may want to remove it to assess what the problem is (be sure to secure permission from the vendor before you do so).

Leaks

THE FIRST THING you'll be looking for inside the boat is evidence of leaks because they always manifest inside rather than outside the boat. Leaks usually show up through staining of one sort or another so be alert to signs of discolouration in the woodwork, linings or fabrics. On a wooden boat any leaks in the deck planking are revealed by staining of the paintwork around the seam, provided that there is no lining in place. Here you can quickly pinpoint the location of the leak, although do remember that water can travel along a seam before it decides to exit to the interior; you may discover a leak on the inside but you'll probably have to move

outside to fix it. There shouldn't be any leaks in steel or aluminium construction boats, so your search is narrowed to fittings or bolt holes, which you should examine for corrosion.

Your task is made more difficult when surveying a composite boat for leaks because while the moulding is usually fully intact, meaning leaks only occur around fittings and securing points that pierce the moulding, a leak through the gel coat on the outside might travel a little way through the moulding before it exits inside the boat. Therefore you'll need to trace it back to its source, which could be some way from the stain.

Evidence of leaks on a deck or superstructure with sandwich construction should ring alarm bells because it could suggest that water has entered the laminate and caused delamination. The deck 'bouncing' test should help to confirm this (see page 52).

↓ *Sprayed-on foam lining inside a steel hull.*

MASTS AND RIGGING

THE ELECTRICAL SYSTEM

THE INTERIOR

SAFETY EQUIPMENT

RIBS AND TENDERS

THE TEN MINUTE SURVEY

AFTER THE SURVEY

You have to appreciate that on a boat any water flying about in lively seas can be travelling upwards rather than the expected downwards travel of rain. When new boats are tested at the builder's yard on completion they may be put under a spray to check for adequate sealing but a high pressure hose test might be more appropriate and more like offshore conditions. Therefore careful checking for staining around all the openings is important.

WINDOWS/PORTHOLES

Sailboats tend to have their portholes in the sides of the coachroof rather than the hull itself, but with motorboats the trend is to fit larger and larger windows and/or portholes in the topsides of the hull, which creates a greater potential for leaks. They tend to be glued and sealed in place, so you'll want to check the condition of the seal and make sure that it is fully intact and free of cuts, nicks or any other rubber deterioration which would reduce its effectiveness. Be alert to evidence showing that sealant has been applied around the window frames and the windows themselves, since this may indicate past

↑ The staining around the window frames on this neglected boat suggests leaking.

↑ This plastic window has crazed but is probably still secure.

← Inspect the window seals even on this modern saloon window.

146

leaks which have been temporarily cured.

Sailboat windows in the coachroof can take a lot of punishment when spray or solid water washes over them and it's a challenge to waterproof opening windows against this punishment. On older boats with poorly designed windows that may have originally been designed for caravan use, the only real solution is to remove the windows and replace them with something of modern marine design, clearly a major (not to mention expensive) job. Therefore, be alert to any colour changes in the varnish around wooden boat windows, which usually indicates a leak.

DOORS

Exterior doors are also a challenge: trying to get an adequate seal around the companionway door in the cockpit of a sailboat can be tricky. Those openings that are closed off by a series of tapered panels of wood never seal completely, although they are usually designed to be at least rainproof. Hinged wooden doors are much the same and both of these types of closure are installed as far as possible in locations where they will not be subject to heavy seas.

On a small sailboat the openings to the accommodation could be subject to solid water in very rough conditions, particularly in following seas, and it seems acceptable that a certain amount of water will find its way through these openings. You will probably see evidence of this in any discolouration around the door area and you'll probably have to accept this because there is no easy cure.

Motorboat doors opening into the cockpit are generally well protected from the elements, particularly those where

↑ Watertight doors are found on larger yachts and the seals need to be examined.

there is a step up into the saloon from the cockpit. Where cockpit and saloon are on a level there can be a risk of water entering via the doorway if, say, the cockpit drains clog up. At the very least there should be a sill at the bottom of the door which raises the level of the entrance above that of the cockpit deck.

OTHER OPENINGS

In addition to window and door openings there is a need for ventilation of some sort, which demands an opening, such as mushroom or dorade vents on the coachroof top. Then there are hatches, which are a vital piece of safety equipment since they are an alternative means of

MASTS AND RIGGING

THE ELECTRICAL SYSTEM

THE INTERIOR

SAFETY EQUIPMENT

RIBS AND TENDERS

THE TEN MINUTE SURVEY

AFTER THE SURVEY

↑ A deck hatch might look fine from the outside but check inside as well.

↓ The inside of a deck hatch showing signs that water is entering in the corners.

↑ A deck hatch with no adjustment on the hinges to allow for when the seal gets worn.

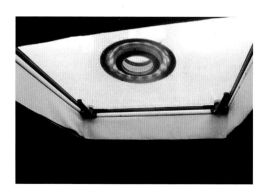

escape from the accommodation in the event of a fire below. Hatches are also used on sailboats as a means of getting sails below or getting them up and they can provide ventilation in good conditions. Ideally a hatch should be raised above deck level so that water cannot lie around the hatch seal, but on sailboats a flush deck can be a desirable feature. Hatches are like portholes and have a rubber seal against which the hatch is clamped, but to get an effective seal you ideally need clamps around the periphery of the hatch. In practice you will normally have

just two clamps on the side away from the hinges and over time the seal can deteriorate when the hatch lid does not seal adequately on the hinge side. To cope with this problem the hatch seal may be soft and have considerable flexibility, so in all cases the seal needs careful checking to ensure continuity and adequate sealing. Once again any staining around the hatch on the inside could be evidence of leaking.

SKIN FITTINGS

You will have already crawled around in the bilges when inspecting them, but be sure to look at the skin fittings to check for leaks, since there is always the risk of leaks around any hull piercing. If there is staining around bilges bolted in with a flange, it may indicate that the bolts themselves are leaking. The bolts around the flange should be an adequate enough seal but some builders have been known to glass in over the top of the flange and its bolts to be doubly sure; it sounds like dedication to the cause of preventing leaks but it actually makes for a very difficult job if the skin fitting has to be replaced at any time.

You'll also need to inspect the log and echo sounder transducer skin fittings, since they have a hull piercing. These are usually fitted with an outside flange that is screwed up tight against an inside flange nut, rather than a flange with separate bolts. Any leaks in the flanges are usually revealed by staining, particularly in a steel hull where the staining could be corrosion.

The best evidence of a leak is water in the bilges, although the boat needs to be afloat to reveal this. There is no reason for water to be in the bilges under normal conditions, except possibly with a wooden hull where there is usually some amount of seepage along the seams. Therefore, if you find it you'll need to seek out its source; it could be a leak from the engine cooling, seepage from a skin fitting or even rain water finding its way inside, but whatever it is you need to identify the cause and cure it.

Delamination and rot

THERE USED TO be a time when builders used solid wood to outfit boat interiors, but today much of the interior is constructed from cheaper panels that are veneered to create a high quality look. Most modern veneers work fine and should be durable but when veneers were first used builders employed cheaper materials and processes, and these haven't always

↓ *The bilge pumps should be part of your interior check.*

→ *Look behind the surface when you are checking the interior.*

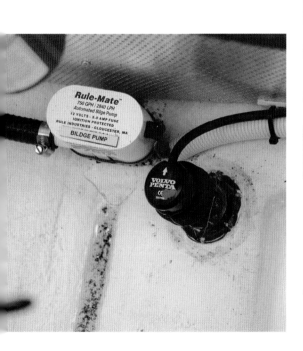

MASTS AND RIGGING

THE ELECTRICAL SYSTEM

THE INTERIOR

SAFETY EQUIPMENT

RIBS AND TENDERS

THE TEN MINUTE SURVEY

AFTER THE SURVEY

stood the test of time in the often damp conditions of a boat. Furthermore, because of the enclosed nature of boats and lack of fresh air circulation they can be a breeding ground for many nasties that will lead to deterioration. Bulkhead panels seem to be particularly susceptible to delamination, so look closely at veneered areas where the bulkheads or panelling abuts the boat hull, especially edges and adjacent areas of panelling. Delamination should be clearly visible and may be discoloured but if you run your hand over the area you may also feel the slight waviness that indicates the start of the process. If you can lift the edge of the veneer you may be able to see the material underneath, which on cheaper boats could be MDF or even chipboard, and if damp has got in, you may see swelling of this material. Once it has taken hold to this extent there is no easy cure, short of replacing the whole panel.

On older boats the interior would be constructed upon a wooden framework that was attached to the hull members and because this wood framework was mainly hidden from view, a cheaper and possibly less durable wood would often be used, making it prone to rot. Because it is hidden away in areas that may be damp and where there is limited or no air circulation this wood can be a starting point for wet rot, and in a worst-case scenario dry rot. Wet rot can be cured by replacement but dry rot could mean stripping out much of the interior and rebuilding. Therefore, try to get access to all the wood framing behind the smart interior panelling and view any sign of discoloured wood with suspicion.

More modern boat interiors tend to have composite mouldings at their base, which should create a more durable structure. These inner mouldings may be laminated into the hull or, in the modern

← *You can see wrinkles in the veneered surface of this door suggesting that delamination is occurring.*

↑ *It is not always easy to get access to parts of the interior.*

these internal structures are not a serious problem as far as the integrity of the boat is concerned and the boat should still be adequately seaworthy, but in actual fact fixing them can mean a major reconstruction of the interior, which can be a daunting prospect, so be sure to examine them closely throughout.

↑ Pay particular attention to areas of the interior where there is water present.

↑ Foam cushions can be susceptible to damp.

technique, glued into place. Check to see that this bonding is still secure as a composite hull can flex whereas the inner moulding may not flex to the same degree or in a different way, and it is the bonding that tends to give way to absorb this movement.

Even modern inner mouldings may still have bulkheads constructed from plywood panels which are bonded to the hull, or on metal boats bolted to the frames. Therefore, again the components may be subject to different movement characteristics, so the joining point between hull and bulkhead wants close inspection. You may think that defects in

SOFT FURNISHINGS

While you have the cushions and furnishings out of the boat, take the opportunity to examine them too. Depending on what sort of foam has been used in the cushions you may find they are heavier than you expect, which could indicate they have absorbed water. Open cell foam acts like a sponge, even in damp conditions, and you can never really get them dry again. If you do need to replace cushions, seek advice from a marine upholsterer as there are so many different types of foam available today. Check any other fabric, such as curtains and blankets, for discolouration which could indicate a hidden leak.

MASTS AND RIGGING

THE ELECTRICAL SYSTEM

THE INTERIOR

SAFETY EQUIPMENT

RIBS AND TENDERS

THE TEN MINUTE SURVEY

AFTER THE SURVEY

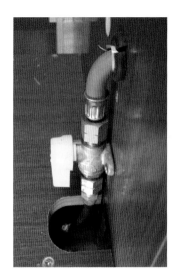

← The galley area should be given careful checks because it is here that you have both water and gas supplies.

→ Joints in the gas supply system should be bubble tested for leaks.

Gas and electrics

GALLEYS VARY ENORMOUSLY in size and sophistication and on modern boats that have generators you'll probably find all the comforts of home, including an electric hob and oven, which obviously pose a fire risk. Short of getting an electrician in, there's very little you can do to test the equipment and its wiring during a survey, but since this type of installation is likely to be as reliable as that in a house you only need check that each item is working.

Where there is no generator, it is often gas that feeds both the stove and fridge, creating the risk of a gas leak. If gas finds its way into the bilges it will lie there, since it is heavier than air, and it only needs a spark, perhaps from an electrical contact, to set off an explosion. Therefore you'll need to check two things: first, that there is a gas detector installed in the bilges and that it is working; this is usually indicated by a warning light on the detector itself and some will emit a beep if the battery is low. Second, you'll need to check that the gas

system itself is sound and gas cannot leak (prevention is always better than cure).

The gas bottle will be stowed in a locker, usually at the stern, where it is isolated from the main compartments of the hull. This locker should be gas tight apart from the access hatch and there should be drain holes leading overboard so that any leak from the gas bottle or its connections will drain overboard rather than into the bilge. There should be a shut off valve connected to the system in the locker so that the gas bottle can be isolated when the gas supply is not required. Ideally the locker should be dedicated to storing the gas supply alone: if other equipment is rattling around in there it could damage the connecting pipes and valves. The bottle should be secure in its mounting and the drain holes open and free. Check the fitting on the gas cylinder for corrosion, since fittings of this type are rarely designed specifically for the marine environment. Check the pipework and valves by brushing them with soapy water with the gas supply turned on; any bubbles will indicate a leak.

Follow the connecting hose – usually a copper pipe with some flexible connections of a rubber type hose – from the gas bottle to the stove, along its length as best you can to ensure it is adequately secured because so often you see these pipes just wandering along in the bilges. The flexible sections need much closer inspection because this is generally where leaks can materialise. The hose must be of the special type suitable for gas and the surface should be free from defects. If there is enough flexibility in the pipe, bend it to see if surface cracks have developed

and pay particular attention to the section that connects with the stove if the stove is mounted on gimbals, as is often the case in sailboats. The constant flexing of this relatively hard rubber pipe can lead to deterioration. Where you can get access also check the connections with the soapy water leak test with, of course, the gas supply turned on. You could give the same treatment to the stove itself, although these are usually very reliable and there should be cut-offs fitted to cut the gas if the flame is not alight. Modern stoves are well covered in this respect but older

→ *Bending a gas hose should not reveal any cracking in the rubber.*

↓ *This gas bottle is stowed in a locker with other equipment, which is not good practice.*

↘ *(bottom right) This gas cylinder is stowed in the rope locker, which is not advisable.*

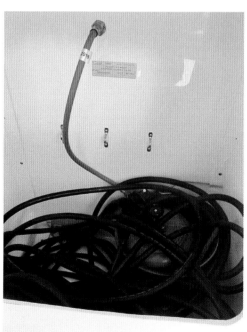

MASTS AND RIGGING

THE ELECTRICAL SYSTEM

THE INTERIOR

SAFETY EQUIPMENT

RIBS AND TENDERS

THE TEN MINUTE SURVEY

AFTER THE SURVEY

equipment might not have these safety cut-offs fitted.

Since there is a fire risk around the galley area it should be free from combustible materials as far as possible. Things like curtains hanging down near the stove can be a hazard, and there may have been stowages added over time. On small and perhaps very old boats you may even find paraffin (kerosene) stoves that work on the Primus principle. These are relatively safe as far as the fuel is concerned but the risk comes in lighting them, and it is doubtful whether insurance companies would take kindly to this type of stove these days.

When it comes to electronic equipment on board there is not a lot you can check except to see that it is working. Modern electronics are generally so reliable that all you need do is switch them on and everything should light up. Where you may find trouble is with the antenna cables such as those for the TV, the GPS, the radar and the VHF radios. These are normally

↑ Navigation equipment in the cockpit is very exposed.

carefully hidden away on a motorboat but on a sailboat the wires will probably go up the mast with connections at deck level, so these connections should be checked for signs of corrosion inside and damage to the exterior wires and fittings.

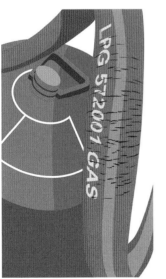

← Cracks showing in the gas hose will mean it is time for replacement.

→ Clips and connection in the gas supply pipes should come in for careful scrutiny.

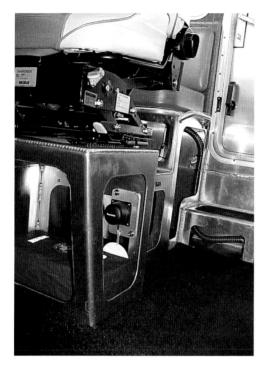

Interior

☐ Are there signs of leaks around windows and hatches?
☐ Is there delamination or rippling of veneer finishes?
☐ Is there access to hidden areas?
☐ Are cushions damp?
☐ Is the gas stove okay?
☐ Are the gas piping and bottles okay?
☐ Is there under floor piping and wiring?
☐ Is there adequate stowage?

← It is worth inspecting seat mountings for security.

↓ This helm station looks in fine condition but ensure you look at it closely.

MASTS AND RIGGING

THE ELECTRICAL SYSTEM

THE INTERIOR

SURVEY CHECKLIST

SAFETY EQUIPMENT

RIBS AND TENDERS

THE TEN MINUTE SURVEY

AFTER THE SURVEY

11 SAFETY EQUIPMENT

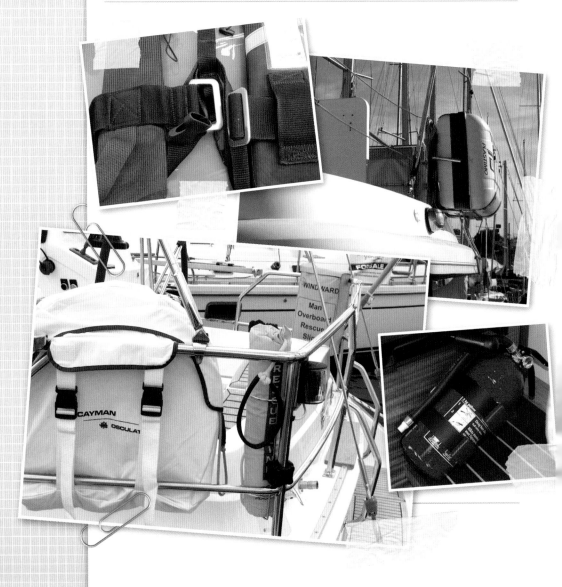

THE VERY ACT of surveying a boat is done with the interest of safety in mind, and if you resolve any problems you find, in theory you shouldn't need the safety equipment. However, nothing is certain at sea so the safety equipment check is a vital part of any survey.

Anchor, line and shackles

THE ANCHOR AND its line should be considered a vital part of safety equipment as it may be your last resort if your engine or sails fail. In most cases it will be constructed from galvanised steel, although only part of the line may be chain and the rest of it rope. Check galvanised steel for corrosion, which will occur when the galvanising has worn away. You will probably see signs of surface corrosion on both the anchor itself and the length of chain closest to the anchor, i.e. the part that drags along the seabed, which is unlikely to be of any consequence (except to leave nasty rust stains on deck if that is where you stow the anchor). So as far as anchor wear and tear is concerned, you need to examine the bearings of any moving parts and the nips of the chain (the inside of the links where one link rubs against another).

To carry out these checks everything must be slack so that you can 'waggle' the moving bits of the anchor. What you are looking for is any excessive play between the moving parts and whether there is still adequate metal left to maintain the required strength. Look for wear in the nips of the chain; if the anchor is mainly used on

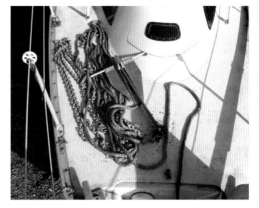

↑ *Get the whole anchor and line on deck for a full check.*

↓ *Corrosion on a galvanised anchor chain may not be serious but check in the nips for wear.*

a sand or gravel bottom, expect quite a lot of wear, while a muddy bottom creates far less abrasion. If there's a dip in the rounded surface of a link, use a pair of callipers to measure it: if it's around ¾ of the original size of an unworn link, it is time to replace the chain. However, anchors and their chains usually have a good safety margin of strength so a fair bit of wear is permissible.

During this inspection, look closely at the shackles that make the connections between the anchor and its chain and those that may be fitted to connect different lengths of chain together. If they are screw shackles the pins of the shackles should be

MASTS AND RIGGING

THE ELECTRICAL SYSTEM

THE INTERIOR

SAFETY EQUIPMENT

RIBS AND TENDERS

THE TEN MINUTE SURVEY

AFTER THE SURVEY

moused, i.e. secured with a piece of wire so that the pin cannot come unscrewed. If the anchor line is a combination of rope and chain, the rope is the weak link and needs to be kept in sound condition, so look for any signs of wear along its length. Take no chances with the rope section; if you feel the time has come for renewal, it is still probably more than adequate for use as a mooring rope. Finally, check that the inboard end is secured down in the chain locker, and preferably at a point where it is accessible with a knife in case you have to slip the anchor line at any time – you don't want to have to enter the chain locker to do that!

Anchor chain is usually made from galvanised steel which can react with aluminium, so the chain should lie on an insulating mat when stowed in an aluminium chain locker. You will probably find that the galvanising has worn off in the first fathom or two from the anchor so that it is rusty. This is normal with a galvanised chain, but the amount of rust could give an indication of the level of usage (and possible need for replacement).

Liferaft, lifejackets and flares

THE LIFERAFT IS an essential piece of kit and offers you a means of escape, but only if it is in working order. You cannot open it up to check it but you can check that it is installed correctly and has been serviced according to the schedule. Servicing used to be on an annual basis but has now been extended to two year intervals, during which the service agent

weighs the inflation bottle and checks the air-holding qualities of the raft. There is usually a service schedule attached to the raft casing in some way to indicate when the last service was carried out. Ensure that the raft is adequately stowed and the painter has been secured to a strong point on board. The method should be a system of straps with a quick release, but it is not uncommon to see a raft lashed down so tightly to the deck that only a sharp knife would free it. Some are even padlocked in place to prevent theft, which is fine in harbour as long as it is unlocked before going to sea. Liferafts may also be stowed in a compartment somewhere around the stern, where they have to be lifted out and thrown overboard. When considering stowage, do bear in mind that liferafts are heavy bits of kit and difficult to handle on

↓ The liferaft should be checked for its service history and condition.

MASTS AND RIGGING

THE ELECTRICAL SYSTEM

THE INTERIOR

SAFETY EQUIPMENT

RIBS AND TENDERS

THE TEN MINUTE SURVEY

AFTER THE SURVEY

a moving boat. Furthermore, if the liferaft can move about, it can suffer wear (for the same reason, there should not be anything else stowed in the same compartment). Check the outside of the raft for any signs of wear and tear which may have extended into the raft itself.

On the other hand, there are no demands for lifejackets to be regularly checked by service agents. To check inflatable jackets, pull hard on all the straps and inspect the stitching to make sure they are in good order and firmly attached. To check lifejackets with gas cylinder inflation, unscrew the metal cylinder and weigh it, in order to determine that there is enough gas for inflation. The difference in weight between a full cylinder and an empty one is quite small so you need a sensitive pair of scales (something like postal scales will do the job). The full weight of the cylinder should be stamped on the outside of the bottle and it is simply a case of checking this weight to confirm that there is still gas in the bottle. While you have the gas cylinder removed, also test the lifejacket's

↑ *Does the liferaft stowage allow for easy launching and is the trigger rope secured?*

↓ *An inflatable type of lifejacket is a good compromise between comfortable wear and effectiveness.*

159

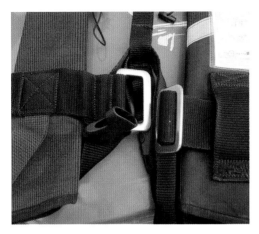

↑ Inspect the state of the stitching on a lifejacket.

operating mechanism by pulling the cord and checking that the firing pin works. Finally, manually inflate the lifejacket through the tube and leave it for a few hours to check that it is holding air. Then put it all back together and you have a lifejacket that should work for the next year or so.

More sophisticated inflatable lifejackets have an automatic system that inflates the lifejacket when it is immersed in water. You can still do the cylinder weighing and manual inflation tests, but there is no easy way to check the automatic system. However, the lifejacket will still operate manually even if the automatic system is defective.

There should be distress flares on board as a requirement and you can check them with a visual inspection. They should be clean and free of any signs of damage. Check the date of manufacture or expiry date, which should be clearly labelled; flares are normally given a four year life span, after which they need replacing.

Fire safety

FIRE IS A nasty experience at sea so you need the means on board to tackle it. While a bucket with a lanyard is one of the

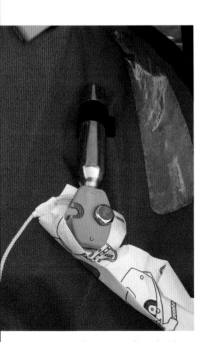

↑ The connected gas bottle.

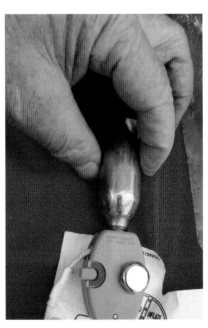

↑ Unscrewing the gas bottle for checking.

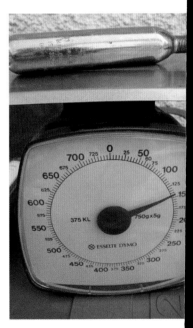

↑ Weighing the gas bottle on postal scale

160

↑ *A large fire extinguisher like this could be difficult to handle on a moving boat.*

best fire-fighting tools to have on board a small boat, the regulations demand you carry adequate fire extinguishers. They come in many shapes and sizes but for boat use they should be small enough to operate one-handed, because you need to secure yourself with the other hand if the boat is rolling about. Most fire extinguishers are designed for use on land and have steel containers and fittings, so your inspection should check for signs of corrosion. There may be a gauge on the extinguisher to show that it is up to pressure (the needle should be in the green), while other fire extinguishers can be checked by weighing

them. You should find the appropriate instructions on the outside of the container and most extinguishers should be serviced every year or two. There are plenty of specialised firms that can do this for you but as they are also in the business of supplying new extinguishers, their checks may not always be unbiased. If you have the instructions, you can do the checks yourself. Finally, fire extinguishers should be located by the exit door of a compartment so that you can get to them without actually entering the burning area.

The engine compartment and galley are the most likely sources of fire, unless you allow smoking down below. You may find your boat or the one you are assessing has a fixed extinguishing system installed in the engine compartment, allowing you to remotely activate the system without having to open the compartment, thereby containing the flames. It is, of course, essential that it is in good working order; there may be instructions for its maintenance on board but the main thing to check is the operating cables or electrical operating system. Some have

↑ *A one-handed fire extinguisher ready for use.*

MASTS AND RIGGING

THE ELECTRICAL SYSTEM

THE INTERIOR

SAFETY EQUIPMENT

RIBS AND TENDERS

THE TEN MINUTE SURVEY

AFTER THE SURVEY

a simple wire pull activation system, so check the wire is not frayed, corroded or kinked to ensure it will actually work when triggered. There should also be covers for the engine compartment air inlets so that you can effectively seal the compartment before triggering the extinguisher. You only get one chance to use these installed systems when there is a fire so you want to get it right first time.

Auxiliary equipment

SAILBOATS IN PARTICULAR often have a variety of auxiliary safety equipment such as marker buoys and lifebuoys for man-overboard situations. These can be

↓ *Man-overboard equipment should be ready for immediate deployment.*

↑ *Emergency equipment should be stowed in good condition and ready for use.*

checked out visually to ensure there are no obvious defects and any rope attachments tested for strength and security.

If there is a radar reflector it will most likely be mast mounted, making it impossible to check in detail, so just ensure that it is still securely attached in the correct orientation. We covered bilge pumps in detail in chapter 7, but they are an important part of the safety equipment, so be sure to lift the float switch and check that the pump is running and that there is no debris in the bilges that could clog the pump.

As with most things you check during a survey, it is easy to rush and merely glance at the equipment. But do bear in mind that it is worth taking the time to thoroughly test your safety equipment – your life may depend on it.

↑ A lifebuoy should be checked for sound condition.

↓ This radar reflector is not mounted upright where it would be most effective.

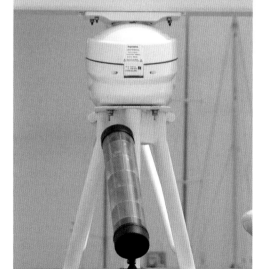

Safety equipment

- ☐ Is the liferaft servicing up to date?
- ☐ Is liferaft stowage suitable?
- ☐ Are lifejacket harnesses in working order?
- ☐ Are lifejacket gas bottles full?
- ☐ Have you tested lifejacket inflation?
- ☐ Are flares up to date?
- ☐ Are fire extinguishers checked and in date?
- ☐ Have you tested lifebuoys and other equipment?

MASTS AND RIGGING

THE ELECTRICAL SYSTEM

THE INTERIOR

SAFETY EQUIPMENT

RIBS AND TENDERS

THE TEN MINUTE SURVEY

AFTER THE SURVEY

SURVEY CHECKLIST

12 RIBS AND TENDERS

THE TENDER IS an important piece of equipment; it not only enhances the cruising experience but helps to ensure you get safely back on board after an evening ashore. Despite this, the tender is often the poor relation when it comes to surveying a boat and it is rarely included in the full report. But while the hard-hulled rigid tender is durable and will stand some neglect, it is often all that stands between you and a serious soaking when returning to your yacht at night in a crowded harbour, so some maintenance and regular checking is advisable.

Today, most tenders are based on RIBs with a hard hull surrounded by an inflatable tube, so for this reason we'll focus on how to survey RIBs, mostly outboard powered, including stand-alone cruising and sports models as well as those used as yacht tenders.

↑ Yacht tenders can have a hard life and suffer neglect.

↓ Check the condition of the towing attachments on an inflatable tender.

MASTS AND RIGGING

THE ELECTRICAL SYSTEM

THE INTERIOR

SAFETY EQUIPMENT

RIBS AND TENDERS

THE TEN MINUTE SURVEY

AFTER THE SURVEY

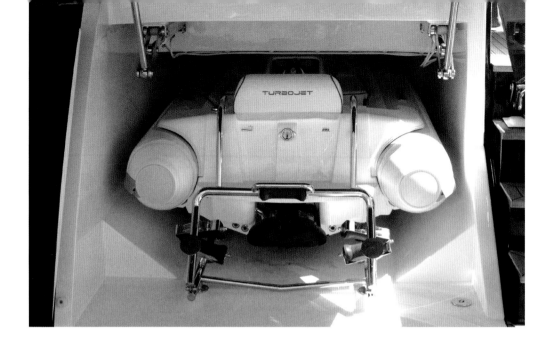

Back from sea

RIBS AND TENDERS will lead a harder life than normal boats; by their very nature, they tend to come in for some serious abuse, bouncing off quays, jetties and other boats and operating off sand and shingle beaches. It's therefore important to survey the boat regularly. You can do a full survey on an annual basis but it's well worth going through a quick routine check every time the boat comes back in from sea. Not only will you discover any damage or wear before it gets serious, but perhaps equally importantly you'll be secure in the knowledge that the boat is ready for sea next time you come to use it.

↓ *This tender looks like it has been abandoned for the winter.*

↓ *It is often the underside of a tender that suffers the most.*

← A tender in a garage should be well protected. Make sure you look for chafe.

→ The seating in a RIB tender can suffer from wear and tear.

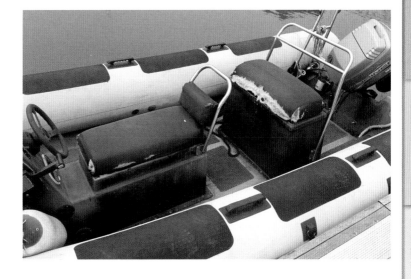

If you have been to the beach, first wash down the boat to remove abrasive dirt and grit. Focus particularly on the area where the air tube is attached to the rigid deck, since the fabric proofing can rub off here, creating the possibility of air leaks. Use a bucket of water and mild detergent, perhaps washing-up liquid, before rinsing down with a hose. While this removes any

↓ The inflatable tubes tend to be the weak point on RIB tenders.

grease and other contaminants from the rubber, it also forces you to examine the tube more carefully, during which time you may discover patches or tape starting to lift away. Moreover, be alert to detergent bubbles gathering at a particular point: this could indicate an air leak.

Next, take the time to check fittings and fixtures. Look inside the console if there is one to ensure the electrics are free of damp, and if there are any exposed connections spray them with a silicone grease aerosol to keep corrosion at bay. Treat any moving parts, such as catches, with the same spray but do not use this spray on the air valves in the tubes or other threaded components because it tends to attract dust and grit, which may clog the screw thread (avoid getting this spray on the tube material, since the silicone can make repairs difficult). While these quick checks reduce problems at sea, you'll also find the annual survey runs more smoothly if you keep on top of tender maintenance throughout the year.

MASTS AND RIGGING

THE ELECTRICAL SYSTEM

THE INTERIOR

SAFETY EQUIPMENT

RIBS AND TENDERS

THE TEN MINUTE SURVEY

AFTER THE SURVEY

The annual survey

FOR THE ANNUAL survey you'll want to strip down the boat as far as possible to get access to hidden parts; for example, it may be possible to remove the console and open up the hatch covers or deck panels.

↑ Securing ropes or straps can chafe the inflatable tube.

↓ The lifting points on a davit stowed tender need careful checking for integrity.

HULL AND AIR TUBES

On modern RIBs and tenders you are unlikely to find many wooden components but wooden transoms were very much in vogue on earlier RIBs. The transom was bonded to the composite hull moulding and tube, so look carefully at these points to ensure the bonding is still intact, otherwise water may get in and separation of the two may escalate. There is usually a doubling piece of plywood over the area where the outboard motor is clamped on and this might be showing signs of wear. There is often just a small bit of movement in the clamping points unless they are done up very tightly so some signs of movement may be visible. This is much more likely to be found with a larger clamped outboard, say up to 40hp, but after that outboards tend to be bolted onto the transom, making them much less prone to slight movement.

On those larger RIBs where the outboard is bolted on check around the bolt holes for any signs of water entry into the laminate or wood (this will be much easier if you remove the engine). The area around the

bolts is highly stressed so check for cracks in the gel coat. You will often find that the transom of larger RIBs looks to be an integral part of the hull moulding, but there may be a plywood insert inside the outer skin that creates a transom of the desired thickness, so check this for water damage. Since the lifting rings are a critical part of the boat, give them a close inspection: Is the laminate to which they are attached in sound condition and free of cracks?

The techniques for surveying tender hulls are much the same as those for composite hulls (see chapter 3). However, with a RIB that has worked off a beach there is likely to be a much higher incidence of chips and scratches, so you need to differentiate between shallow gel coat damage, which is more or less cosmetic, and deeper damage, where the underlying laminate is showing through. Check any abrasion along the keel at the bow and look for cracks in the gel coating, which could indicate impact damage (you are more likely to find these on a RIB that operates off a trailer).

As far as the air tubes and the fabrics of the boat are concerned, go over the surface with a fine-tooth comb just like you would with any hull, looking for areas where the outer proofing of the fabric has worn away and/or the taping and seals have lifted, and any other evidence of damage or decay. It usually helps to deflate the tube so you can get into the areas that are usually inaccessible, particularly the area inside where the tube attaches to the

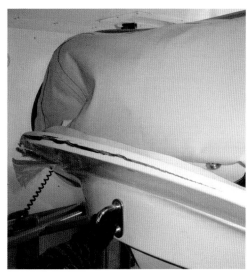

↑ *Bow collision damage on a RIB tender.*

← *Time for a full overhaul.*

MASTS AND RIGGING

THE ELECTRICAL SYSTEM

THE INTERIOR

SAFETY EQUIPMENT

RIBS AND TENDERS

THE TEN MINUTE SURVEY

AFTER THE SURVEY

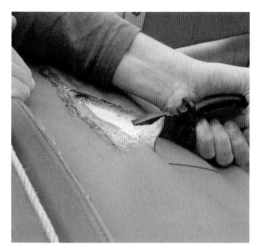

↑ *Pulling off a poorly applied patch with pliers.*

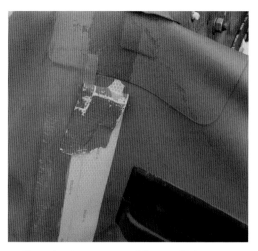

↑ *The sealing tapes are one of the most likely points to need attention on an inflatable.*

hull in a tight vee: this can be prone to damage and wear if sand or stones have lodged in the space.

You may find regions where the outer layer of fabric proofing has worn away through abrasion, for example if a mooring line or some other fixture passes over or rubs on the tube. Wear in this outer layer is usually not too serious, but it may need patching up because the sandwiched woven fabric squeezed between the inner and outer layers of rubber can start to absorb water and cause delamination. 'Wicking' (where the pressurised air inside the tubes is forced along minute channels within the reinforcing woven fabric, only to find its way out at an outside seam) is also a problem on inflated tubes; it is one of the reasons behind the thin tape glued over the outside seams, which is intended to prevent the air escaping and thus water finding its way into the fabric. Check for lifts and leaks along these seams.

Pay particular attention to the point where the air tube is glued to the rigid

section of the hull. This area is under a lot of strain and on the outside of the hull there can be a strong peeling action where the water flows upwards and away from the hull when operating in waves. Glued attachments are the norm for this connection but there are alternatives, such as the tube being bolted on through doubling plates which creates a form of sail track system where the tube attachment points slide on. For these types of attachment you only need check for any impact damage from coming alongside too hard.

During your detailed inspection of the tubes check such items as handholds, fender strips, bow rings and transoms. Pick at the edge with your fingernail: you shouldn't be able to lift it at any of the joints, seams or patches. If you do find any areas of lifting or wear and tear mark them with a magic marker so that they can receive further attention. If the tender is towed, check any rope attachment points, which have a tendency to pull away under the strain.

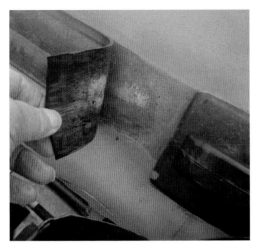

↑ *Here the rubbing strip is coming adrift and needs re-gluing.*

painting it all over the surface. Air leaks will soon become evident through bubbles forming, perhaps in a series or along the edges of a seam. Bubbles appearing over a wider area of fabric indicate that the proofing is porous, which can mean a considerable repair job. Mark any areas where bubbles appear so that you can find them once the tube dries off and before you start repair work.

Paint the detergent solution around air valves, too, to check them for air tightness. The inflation valves in inflatable boats are generally very reliable and if replacements are required it is generally only the insert that needs replacing, which is a straightforward job. A whole valve replacement is probably a job for the service station.

If you're surveying your own RIB you'll probably be aware of whether or not the boat is leaking air during use, but now is a good time to examine the air holding qualities of the entire boat by painting the air tubes with a soft brush dipped in a detergent solution. Inflate the tube hard and then work the solution up into a foam,

If the RIB has been kept afloat, the bottom of the hull will have been coated with antifouling paint to prevent marine growth, which can make detailed inspection more difficult. On some RIB

↓ *A poorly applied patch with excessive glue.*

↓ *The edges of a patch can be lifted with a blunt screwdriver after softening with a hot air gun.*

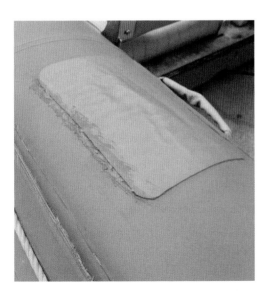

MASTS AND RIGGING

THE ELECTRICAL SYSTEM

THE INTERIOR

SAFETY EQUIPMENT

RIBS AND TENDERS

THE TEN MINUTE SURVEY

AFTER THE SURVEY

↑ The lifting point attachment on this RIB is corroding.

↘ Not much room for access to this RIB engine.

the engine hood should be a warning sign that closer inspection is required (remove the engine hood off and examine the exposed engine). Check the condition of both the anode fitted near the propeller and the internal anode in the cooling water system (if there is one). If the engine is not tilted when the boat is afloat there may be marine growth on the leg of the motor and in the cooling water intake; this should just scrape off, but use a wooden rather than metal implement so as to avoid damaging the paintwork on the engine.

A RIB's outboard motor also tends to get knocked about a bit due to the

designs the tube is set low in relation to the rigid section of the hull so that the lower part of the tube is permanently immersed at rest. Not only does this make the tube attractive to marine growth but you will need to carefully examine the tube joints and seams in the immersed area to ensure there are no signs of damage from the constant immersion.

ENGINE SYSTEMS

If your RIB has a diesel engine a survey will be much the same as detailed in chapter 5. However, most modern tenders and smaller RIBs use an outboard motor, so you will need to take a different approach. The outboard's strength is that it is supplied as a largely self-contained unit beneath a hood, although this does mean it is easier to neglect the engine's systems. Corrosion was quite a problem on earlier outboards because they were constructed from many dissimilar metals, but manufacturers have resolved this for modern units. However, signs of corrosion or salt deposits inside

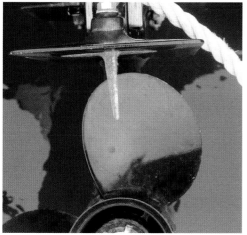

↑ The trim fin on this outboard has been adjusted to counteract the propeller torque.

↑ Follow the handbook instructions when checking an outboard and also check all the pipes and wires coming in.

often violent motion of the boat, so be sure to check the mounting brackets and fastenings on the transom, particularly if it is one of the lifting types that have a multitude of pivot points. With transom mounted outboards check the clamping system or mounting bolts for tightness and any signs of movement and that locking washers or nuts are fitted to securing bolts.

Small outboards up to 5hp often have an integrated fuel tank, which means the fuel system has been fully tried and tested and should be reliable. However, you can still check the piping for leaks and peer into the tank itself to see if there is any sediment in the bottom. Opening up the fuel filter will also show if there is sediment in the system and this applies to both integral and remote fuel tanks.

Some outboards are supplied from a portable fuel tank inside the boat. While these have the advantage that you can take them ashore for refuelling, not to mention they are built for the job and therefore usually reliable, they are difficult to secure.

Secure them tight because it only wants a slight amount of play to get them moving: go for webbing straps with a ratchet tightener, since elastic straps can rarely be secured tight enough to prevent the tanks moving under the motion of the boat. Ensure the flexible pipe that feeds the fuel to the engine is not being pinched, nipped or damaged. Mild steel portable tanks will corrode in a salt atmosphere; plastic

↑ The fuel tank should be securely stowed.

MASTS AND RIGGING

THE ELECTRICAL SYSTEM

THE INTERIOR

SAFETY EQUIPMENT

RIBS AND TENDERS

THE TEN MINUTE SURVEY

AFTER THE SURVEY

173

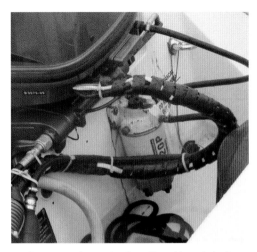

↑ The pipes and wires for the outboard have to be free to move so should be checked for any signs of chafe.

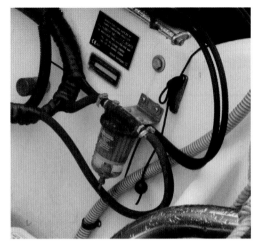

↑ The fuel filter and lines for an outboard.

↓ Loose lines and fuel pipes can be a hazard in a tender.

tanks are the alternative but are not recommended for carrying petrol fuel.

Built-in metal tanks are now the standard for most larger RIBs and they are usually fitted under the deck, making them difficult to access. There may be a deck hatch giving access to the pipe connection plate, so check that everything here is tight and free of any signs of leaks.

Outboard RIBs rarely have a gas detector fitted in the bilges because there shouldn't be electrical connections here to ignite gas, but a sniff in the fuel tank compartment will indicate any signs of leakage (and if you find them, you'll need to check all piping and connections). Check the end fittings on the flexible fuel pipes, usually a push fit with an automatic seal comprising a spring loaded ball valve pressing onto a rubber 'O' ring. This O ring serves to seal the ball valve when the pipe is disconnected and forms the seal when the pipe is connected. A leak through the O ring when the pipe is disconnected may not be particularly serious but any leakage

MASTS AND RIGGING

THE ELECTRICAL SYSTEM

THE INTERIOR

SAFETY EQUIPMENT

RIBS AND TENDERS

THE TEN MINUTE SURVEY

AFTER THE SURVEY

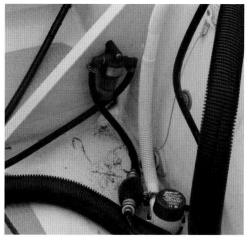

↑ *Check all the corners and systems on a tender for reliability.*

of manual or electric starting. With manual starting you might not require an electric supply or battery, so in this case simply check the starter cord for any signs of wear or chafe which could indicate that it's time for renewal. Larger RIB engines do require an electrical supply, which will need checking (see chapter 9). In particular, examine the heavy duty cables that take the battery supply connection to the outboard as these will move under steering movements (these cables, the control and perhaps the fuel supply pipes are often contained within an outer tube to reduce the chances of chafing and damage).

when the pipe is connected immediately allows air to be sucked into the engine rather than fuel, meaning the engine will stop, or much more likely it won't start in the first place. Therefore, carefully check all O rings for signs of damage.

From the fuel line the fuel is routed first into a fuel filter and then into a carburetor or fuel injection system. On some installations there may be a fuel filter mounted external to the engine, often on the transom where it is clearly visible, and this serves to trap any dirt in the fuel and also to separate out any water that might be in the fuel. The glass bulb on these filters provides a ready check for any contamination in the fuel. The engine mounted fuel filter may also have a glass bulb so that it can be checked quickly for contamination.

ELECTRICAL SYSTEMS

An outboard motor also requires an electrical supply. For smaller outboard motors up to about 50hp you have a choice

Tenders

SURVEY CHECKLIST

- ☐ Is the air tube holding air?
- ☐ Are tapes or patches lifting away on the air tube?
- ☐ Are the davit mountings secure?
- ☐ Are the tender lifting points secure?
- ☐ Are there chips or damage to the rigid hull?
- ☐ Are the fuel tank and battery secure?
- ☐ Is the outboard secure on the transom?
- ☐ Is all the equipment on board/ working?

13 THE TEN MINUTE SURVEY

WHEN YOU ARE in the market for a new or replacement boat you will often go around a prospective purchase with the owner or broker in tow. Obviously he/she will be pointing out the good bits while you'll be looking at it from the point of view of, 'Will it suit me? What needs doing?' Presumably you've done your homework before contacting the broker or private seller and have some idea of the type and make of boat you are after. This would suggest that the boat you are looking at now is close to your requirements and you want to assess its condition before buying it. An advertisement may say that the boat is in 'good condition' but exactly what does 'good condition' mean? It may look smart and clean but most sellers tart up their boat before selling it. What you really want to know is: Are there any major

↓ *You would not need ten minutes to check this one out.*

↑ *Ropes in poor condition like this could suggest a casual approach to general maintenance.*

MASTS AND RIGGING

THE ELECTRICAL SYSTEM

THE INTERIOR

SAFETY EQUIPMENT

RIBS AND TENDERS

THE TEN MINUTE SURVEY

AFTER THE SURVEY

↑ *The first impression here is that the boat is in good condition.*

problems with this particular boat that may only become apparent after you've purchased it?

This is where the 'ten minute survey' comes in: it gives you some idea of what to look for when you first tour the boat with the broker or seller. Obviously you will be paying attention to all of the good points the broker points out but at the same time you can be making an assessment of the general condition of the boat. In ten minutes it is possible to get an idea of the condition of a boat – not in detail of course, but it could be a sort of make or break point in the purchase process. In some ways this is a negative survey, not so much learning what on the boat is in good condition but whether it has suffered damage in the past or has been through a period of neglect. While the ten minute survey won't give you any sort of guarantee that the boat is in sound condition, it could provide you with enough information to decide whether to look at the boat in more detail and then proceed to paying for a professional surveyor's report, or walk away.

Before your visit

BEFORE YOU EVEN go to see the boat you'll need to research the particular class you have in mind; the more you can find out about the boat before you visit it the better because you'll have a strong foundation for your ten minute survey.

Over the past 40 years boats have tended to be built in series production, meaning there will be a number of similar models. This means that you should be able to search the internet to find out how the boat is constructed, and with a composite boat you will want to know whether it is a sandwich hull or solid laminate and what materials were used. You'll often find an owner's club for a particular class of boat, especially sailboats, which may include a forum on which owners speak about their problems and experiences with the boat. This can be a valuable source of information for defects that develop over time and the owners' solutions. If the forum throws up a list of sad stories you may be put off buying the boat, but at least it gives you a starting point for your survey when you visit it. On the flip side do be wary of comments from existing owners, since they may be biased when trying to justify their purchase decision.

You can also find information about the construction of a boat from the builder, if they are still in business. Most builders are willing to share the specifications of older boats, which can be a tremendously useful starting point.

If you are contemplating the purchase of a one-off design, the boat is usually constructed in wood or metal. You may not have access to detailed information about the materials used, so instead do a little research into the reputation of the builder, on boating forums rather than his own website. If it is a steel boat you'll want to know about the quality of the steelwork and, equally important, the paint systems used to prevent corrosion. If it is a wooden

↑ *Ask yourself are the rudder and keel in line?*

construction you'll want to know the type of wood used, since different woods have varying levels of durability.

The survey

ALL SURVEYS SHOULD start in the same way, and that is to examine the boat from afar, then walk around it; you're looking for anything that seems out of place on a well ordered boat. If it's a sailboat check that the mast is in line with the hull and keel and that everything looks square and in order. For both sail- and motorboats, check the sides, that the stanchions are upright and in line and everything is 'square' and as it should be. Check the navigation lights and antenna.

MASTS AND RIGGING

THE ELECTRICAL SYSTEM

THE INTERIOR

SAFETY EQUIPMENT

RIBS AND TENDERS

THE TEN MINUTE SURVEY

AFTER THE SURVEY

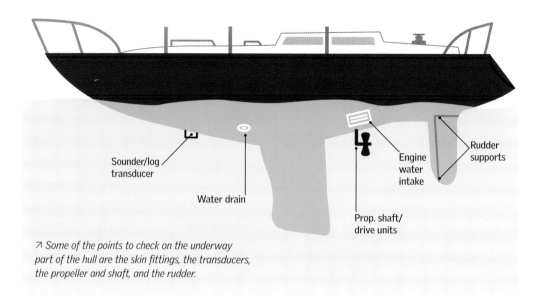

Sounder/log
transducer

Water drain

Engine
water
intake

Rudder
supports

Prop. shaft/
drive units

↗ *Some of the points to check on the underway
part of the hull are the skin fittings, the transducers,
the propeller and shaft, and the rudder.*

OFF BOARD

Now move closer for a more detailed
look at the hull. If you're inspecting a
motorboat it may be possible to get up
close and personal with the topsides but
the underwater parts may be concealed.
With a sailboat it is often the reverse, with
the topsides high above you but the keel
area in clear view. In both cases, you can
at least check the state of the hull finish
– if it is dull, give it a rub to see if there
is gloss underneath the surface grime.
If not, you may find that a powder comes
off on your hand when you rub the surface,
which could mean that the gel coat is
deteriorating and it may be time for a
paint job.

   If the hull is a composite look for any
signs of the gel coat cracking, which could
indicate a heavy coming alongside in the
past or even a collision. With wooden
boats be alert to signs that the seams
between the planking are pushing out;
while not a serious problem in itself, if it

is accompanied by staining or rust streaks
there could be something going on inside,
such as corrosion of the fastenings. Look
for signs of unevenness in the wood surface
or cracks in the gloss finish, which may
indicate wood rot beneath the paint. Ideally
you'd want to test this with a pricker or tap
with a hammer, but if neither is possible
try tapping with a knuckle and if you hear
a soft sound it could indicate soft wood.
However, keep in mind that this is a quick
test and not always fail-safe. If the hull is
steel, be alert to the giveaway rust streaks
of corrosion and if you come across them,
take a closer look to see if there is any
raising of the surface, which could indicate
that the corrosion has set in to a greater
depth. With an aluminium hull there
shouldn't be any signs of corrosion, but
this softer metal can dent easily so look
for fairness in the hull lines.

   With any hull material you want to
place your head as close to the surface
as you can and look along the hull. Here

→ *Broken sections like this can be a guide to the overall general condition of the boat.*

you are checking that the hull remains fair and there are no giveaway signs of repair work, which may show as being slightly out of line with the rest of the hull. On a composite, look at the join between the hull and the deck mouldings to check for any signs of movement between the two or staining emanating from the join. On a sailboat check the join between the hull and the keel for any signs or corrosion or opening up, which should be viewed with suspicion: corrosion here could indicate that the keel bolts, if they are made of steel, are deteriorating, or it could just be corrosion on a cast iron keel. If the gap between the two has opened up slightly it's time to drop the keel and take a closer look. On a motorboat you might have a steel keel band to examine and, again, you're looking for corrosion between the hull and the band. Loose securing bolts may suggest a replacement band is in order; if the boat has a keel band it may indicate that the boat has been lying at a drying

out mooring. Check along the edges of the spray rails and chines on a planing hull, since these are often gel coat-rich areas that are easily chipped.

At the stern try to move the rudder(s) to see if there is any play in the bearings and lift the propeller to check for the same in the shaft bearings. On both fittings you may be able to see whether the bearing holes are elongated through wear (if these parts are visible). Sailboat rudders take a lot of strain so look closely at the rudder surface for signs of cracks or deterioration.

ON BOARD

Now you have used up perhaps three or four minutes of your ten, so it's time to move on board. Walk around the deck looking as closely as you can at the fittings and fixtures. This will particularly apply to sailboats where the fittings can come under a lot of stress, while on motorboats you'll want to focus on the rails and the

MASTS AND RIGGING

THE ELECTRICAL SYSTEM

THE INTERIOR

SAFETY EQUIPMENT

RIBS AND TENDERS

THE TEN MINUTE SURVEY

AFTER THE SURVEY

↑ *The varnish work looks to be in poor condition but try to look a bit deeper than just the cosmetic defects.*

mooring fitting at bow and stern. Here you are looking for any spider-like dark cracks in the gel coat around the fittings and the mounting, which would indicate that they have been under stress at some point. This is quite common with guard rails but if you see it around high stress fittings, such as chain plate anchorages, block tracks and winch or davit bases, it could indicate that there may be some form of trouble lurking within the mounting point of the fitting, which will need serious attention.

If the boat has a wooden deck look for any undue compression of the wood around fittings and any signs such as discolouration, which may indicate that there has been deterioration in that area.

A fully laid wooden deck can be a sign of quality but be sure to check along the seams to ensure the sealing is intact. Many boats today have a plastic imitation wooden deck which will generally remain intact, but look for any signs of lifting or poor bonding around the edges where water could get in below.

Try out the bounce test on the deck and coachroof so you can confirm their rigidity or otherwise. Any feeling of excessive movement may signal that the sandwich construction of the panels is breaking down, but it is difficult to specify what exactly is excessive movement: a normal deck should have very little to no movement. Do the same test in the cockpit

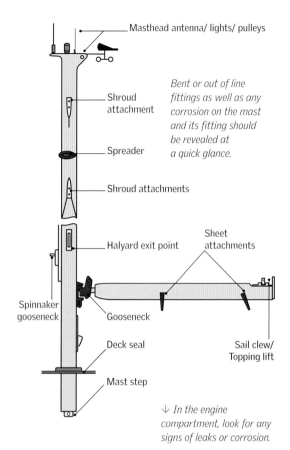

Masthead antenna/ lights/ pulleys

Shroud attachment

Bent or out of line fittings as well as any corrosion on the mast and its fitting should be revealed at a quick glance.

Spreader

Shroud attachments

Halyard exit point

Sheet attachments

Spinnaker gooseneck

Gooseneck

Deck seal

Sail clew/ Topping lift

Mast step

↓ *In the engine compartment, look for any signs of leaks or corrosion.*

of both sail- and motorboats and if you find any movement, look for gel coat cracking in the corners or angles of the moulding.

Next turn your attention to the mast and its fittings. Are there any signs of corrosion where the shroud or other fittings attach to the mast? As far as you can, inspect the attachment points of any high stress fittings and the attachment plate to ensure they are secure and intact. With the rigging screws, is there enough span left on the threads for further tightening and are both port and starboard screws adjusted to about the same position? If not, you may be faced with renewing the rigging or perhaps there is a problem with the mast step which has allowed the mast to drop down slightly. These could all be warning signs of more serious trouble but it will be hard to be specific without much closer examination. Check the condition of the ropes that control the sails for signs of chafe or wear. Even replacing ropes can be an expensive proposition once you have purchased a boat.

The state of the engine compartment is perhaps your best guide for the standard of general maintenance around the boat. Here the need for maintenance and order is concentrated, and it should not take more than a quick look around to confirm the general state of the wiring, the cooling system and the engine and other machinery. Poor quality or badly maintained wiring will show in draped or loose wires (which may also indicate that there have been modifications to the wiring over the years) and corrosion around terminal areas. All wiring should be tidily secured in place. If you can view

MASTS AND RIGGING

THE ELECTRICAL SYSTEM

THE INTERIOR

SAFETY EQUIPMENT

RIBS AND TENDERS

THE TEN MINUTE SURVEY

AFTER THE SURVEY

the batteries, check they are firmly secured and clean and free of corrosion. Check the worm drive securing clips in the cooling system for corrosion; if it is present, it's likely the hoses that the clips secure have not been renewed for some time. You should be able to see the seacocks at the water intakes in the hull bottom and if they too show signs of corrosion, it can signal that general maintenance has not been all it should have been. What is the condition of the exhaust pipe(s) and the engine itself? Is the engine clean and oil free and does it look as though it has had loving care and attention?

Use up any remaining time in your ten minute survey to inspect the boat's interior. Look for signs of discolouration and/or staining around windows, hatches and the

↑ This definitely looks like one to walk away from.

↓ You should be able to get a good indication of the general quality of a boat by looking at the condition of the pipework and fittings.

deck head covering, which could suggest leaks. It's worth opening up a few of the lockers or floor hatches to get a view of the inside of the hull. On a sailboat, prioritise those in the bottom of the boat in order to get a look at what is happening to the keel.

Finally, if you can, try to inspect the steering system for signs of wear and tear or poor maintenance. If you can't get to it easily at least turn the steering wheel or tiller to test if there is any play in the system; a small amount is okay but anything more than a quarter turn should be viewed with suspicion.

Now that you've spent ten minutes touring the boat, it's time to come to a conclusion. What potential defects did you uncover and how does this affect the overall picture? There's bound to be at least a few minor issues on a second hand boat, but if you come across a catalogue of potential faults you have two options: you can walk away and continue your search, or you can try to renegotiate the price, provided of course you have the means to resolve the issues once you've purchased the boat.

Since you've only had a ten-minute look round the boat, you won't be in the strongest position to negotiate; a good broker or owner will already know about any defects you've picked up on and may well say that their price already reflects the condition. If this is the case, you could request a closer look at the areas that are worrying you, and this is where the content of this book really comes into play. If you're still unsure, you could try to negotiate a price 'subject to survey' and bring in the experts. At that point

you'll have a better idea of the condition of the boat and can still walk away should the professional opinion put you off the purchase.

Carrying out you own survey can be quite a lot of hard work and you need to be fairly fit and active. It can also be very rewarding and you will feel happier knowing your boat inside out, or if you are buying, you will have a good idea of just what you are going to get your hands on.

Ten minute survey

- [ ] Are the hull, mast and keel square and in line?
- [ ] Are hull surfaces smooth and fair?
- [ ] Is the engine compartment clean and free of signs of leaks or oil?
- [ ] Are the hoses and connections in good order?
- [ ] Are the deck and coachroof sound?
- [ ] Is there no obvious damage to prop/s and rudder/s?
- [ ] Does the interior smell sweet?
- [ ] Is the interior free of signs of leaks?
- [ ] Is there corrosion on metal hulls?
- [ ] Are the mast and rigging in good order?
- [ ] Do electrics look secure and corrosion free?
- [ ] Are there signs of interior veneers lifting or rippled?

MASTS AND RIGGING

THE ELECTRICAL SYSTEM

THE INTERIOR

SAFETY EQUIPMENT

RIBS AND TENDERS

THE TEN MINUTE SURVEY

AFTER THE SURVEY

SURVEY CHECKLIST

14 AFTER THE SURVEY

SO YOU HAVE spent the afternoon crawling around a boat and looking into all the parts that you do not normally see. Hopefully you have listed all defects and potential fixes, which will become a fantastic resource when you're judging what steps to take next.

If you have surveyed a boat you're thinking of purchasing you'll probably want to adopt much of the negotiating strategy discussed at the end of chapter 13. You might have quite a comprehensive list of potential defects and it makes sense to try and whittle this down to a more manageable length of the major items you feel detract from the value of the boat. You might include the following:

☐ The electrical system is showing signs of corrosion in some areas.
☐ There are gel coat cracks around many of the stanchion bases.
☐ Abrasion marks on the keel suggest the boat has run aground at some point since the last antifouling.
☐ There are signs of corrosion around the keel bolts inside the hull and along the keel/hull join.
☐ The rudder bearings show signs of wear.
☐ The engine cooling water system appears to be in poor condition.
☐ There are signs of leaking around the saloon windows.

You may even go back on board to show what you have found, although, short of dismantling the boat, neither you nor the vendor can be certain of just what is required to fix the problems. This is the time to confirm that you will bring in a professional surveyor for a second opinion, which will enable you to agree a 'price subject to survey', based on what you have discovered during your inspection. If the vendor is being difficult, he will find it much harder to argue with a professional.

Of course, the alternative (and I strongly suggest you take it if a boat looks sad and uncared for) is to walk away from the deal. Call it a gut reaction, but first impressions are rarely ever wrong. After all, it is worth remembering that out at sea your life depends on the reliability of your craft.

You should also bear this in mind during a survey of your own boat. Some owners can become blinkered to severe problems;

I saw one owner rebuilding the interior of an old boat and fixing it to a wooden hull riddled with dry rot, which he chose to ignore, thinking it would fix itself. The only real solution for that particular boat was to set fire to it in order to prevent the rot spreading to other boats in the yard.

If you're finding it difficult to prioritise work that needs doing on your own boat, try separating the defects into several categories: those affecting the safety of the boat at sea, cosmetic problems, those affecting convenience or comfort on board and routine maintenance. By doing this, you can determine which items need to be completed by a boatyard and those you can handle yourself. The latter depends a great deal on time and your skill-set, but there is a lot to be said for doing the work yourself when you can, since you'll learn a great deal about your boat.

There could also be items on your list that don't have an obvious solution – they require further examination and possible stripping of parts to get a closer look. There may be possible corrosion on the keel bolts of a motorboat, or excessive play in the propeller shaft or the rudder bearings. Whatever the issue, let a boatyard tackle the investigations, since they will view the situation objectively.

Surveying your own boat or a potential purchase is a bit like becoming a detective for the day, but as long as you keep good records of everything you uncover, you're more likely to be able to piece the clues together to arrive at a possible solution. You're in a much better position to decide what the next step is, and if that means walking away from a boat, do it: next time you're out at sea and something goes wrong, you won't regret it.

MASTS AND RIGGING

THE ELECTRICAL SYSTEM

THE INTERIOR

SAFETY EQUIPMENT

RIBS AND TENDERS

THE TEN MINUTE SURVEY

AFTER THE SURVEY

187

INDEX